GRACE FOR MOMS

52 Devotions to
Inspire and Encourage

NAPHTALIE VARISTE

Dedication

Thank you to the Most High God for choosing me as a vessel to write this book, which is meant to inspire and encourage both myself and other mothers as we learn to embrace grace from Him, extend it to others, and receive it within ourselves. May these words be used to touch hearts and transform lives.

To my incredible husband, Donald,

Thank you for walking this journey with me and for showing me grace on the days I need it most. Your unwavering support, encouragement, and belief in me have been a constant source of strength. Thank you for pushing me to pursue my dreams and use the gifts God has placed within me. You are my partner and my encourager. I couldn't do this without you. With all my love.

To my precious son Abe, the one who made me a mommy, you are my pride, my joy, and one of my greatest blessings. I love you beyond words.

To the mom walking through the heartache of infertility; to the expecting mom courageously stepping into the unknown; to the working mom balancing countless roles and responsibilities; and to the adoptive, stepmom or foster mom loving and raising children as her own, know this: God sees you. He is with you in every moment, gently guiding your steps and holding you close. May His boundless grace meet you right where you are.

Introduction

Motherhood is one of the most sacred and beautiful callings a woman can embrace. This journey is filled with immeasurable joy and profound love, but it also brings moments of exhaustion, doubt, and overwhelm. In the midst of it all, there is one thing every mother needs: grace.

Grace to rise and try again after a hard day.

Grace to forgive yourself when things don't go as planned.

Grace to love deeply, even when your strength feels spent.

Grace to trust that God is at work, even when you cannot yet see the evidence.

This devotional was created to walk alongside you through every season of motherhood, the highs, the lows, and everything in between. Over the next 52 weeks, you'll find encouragement, inspiration, and gentle reminders of God's unfailing presence in your everyday moments.

My prayer is that these pages will fill your heart with hope and courage. May you be inspired to notice God's hand at work in both the ordinary and extraordinary parts of your family's story. And may you discover renewed joy as you embrace the gift of motherhood, fully covered by His perfect grace.

Let's take this journey together, one week at a time.

With love,

Naphtalie Variste

CHAPTER
ONE

Multiply and Flourish

> 📖 **Genesis 1:28**
>
> *"God blessed them and said to them, 'Be fruitful and increase in number; fill the earth and subdue it.'"*

I often find myself reflecting deeply on this powerful Bible verse. After God created Adam and Eve in His own likeness, His very first command to them was to be fruitful and multiply. The Bible tells us that everything God made was good, and in that goodness, He placed a profound desire in our hearts to see more of humanity flourish on the earth. God loved us so much that He wanted us to fill the world, to walk in dominion and stewardship over His creation.

Not only did God create mankind and place us in the breathtaking Garden of Eden, but He also designed us to bring forth new life. This highlights just how sacred and vital pregnancy and childbirth are in God's eyes. The ability to conceive and nurture a new life is not just a biological process, it is the fulfillment of one of God's divine intentions for humanity.

Of course, we know the journey is not always easy. The hurdles that come with pregnancy and motherhood are real, and sin has made this path more complicated and painful than God originally intended. Yet, despite these hardships, God remains faithful. He loves children deeply and welcomes each new life into His loving embrace.

As women, we are invited to see our children through God's eyes: with joy, and unwavering love. The journey of motherhood looks different for every one of us: some are single moms, others are divorced; some have walked the difficult road of infertility, while others have faced the heartbreak of loss; some stay at home nurturing their children full-time, while others balance the demands of work and family.

Whatever your motherhood story may be, I encourage you this week to pause and reflect on this Bible verse. Write down what it means to you personally. Let it be a source of strength and encouragement through every meltdown, every tantrum, every morning and night routine, every school drop-off and pick-up, through all the chaos in between.

Motherhood is truly a gift, a tangible blessing from God Himself. It is a sacred calling, one that reflects His love and faithfulness in the world.

Prayer:

Heavenly Father,

I come before you with a grateful heart, thanking you for the incredible gift you have bestowed upon women, the blessing of bearing children.

Just as you commanded in your Holy Word to be fruitful and multiply, you have designed women with the sacred ability to bring forth new life.

Thank you for the wonder and miracle of pregnancy, for the strength and grace you provide throughout this journey, and for the joy of nurturing your creation. I honor your divine plan and recognize the sacredness of motherhood, a reflection of your love and faithfulness.

May every child born be a testament to your goodness, and may every mother feel your sustaining presence, peace, and joy as she fulfills this blessed calling.

In Jesus' name. Amen.

Reflections of Grace

✝ How do you see God's call to be fruitful lived out in your role as a mother, both in nurturing your children physically and in helping them grow spiritually?

✝ In what ways has God uniquely gifted and equipped you to guide, protect, and nurture the hearts of your children?

✝ What areas of your motherhood journey might you need to surrender to God so you can walk more fully in His calling for you?

_____

_____

CHAPTER
TWO

The Faithful God: Keeper of Every Promise

📖 **Genesis 21:1-2**

Now the Lord was gracious to Sarah as He had said, and the Lord did for Sarah what He had promised. Sarah became pregnant and bore a son to Abraham in his old age, at the very time God had promised him."

Have you been waiting for God's promise to bear children, wondering when it will finally come true? I've been in your shoes, and I know exactly how that wait feels. I know the pain of being asked, "are you pregnant yet?' The ache of people staring at your belly and seeing no sign of a baby.

I got married at 33, and my husband and I both believed God had called us to be parents, and that it would happen quickly. But it took longer than we expected. What might seem like a short time to some was an eternity to us. Month after month, for six months straight, I hoped this would be the month I'd get pregnant, but it didn't happen. Every time my cycle came, it felt like God's promise was being delayed.

I thank God for His Word and for blessing me with a husband who understood spiritual warfare. With each disappointment, we kept holding on to God's promise. My husband received the revelation to buy diapers and wipes by faith, and we prayed over them, thanking God in advance for our child. Then, when we least expected it, we found out we were pregnant with our baby boy.

This journey takes me back to God's promise to Abraham and Sarah. We serve a faithful God, a God who keeps His Word. It doesn't matter how the world sees us, or how we see ourselves, especially in terms of age or circumstances. If God says it, it will come to pass.

The real test is when it doesn't happen on our timeline, through months or even years of miscarriages, infertility, and waiting. Do we let our circumstances overshadow God's Word? As humans, we're entitled to our feelings, and God meets us there. However, we must remain vigilant, guarding our hearts against surrendering to hopelessness, despair, or doubt in God's promises.

Today, I want to remind you to fully surrender and believe in God's will for your life. If He has called you to be a mom, it doesn't matter what the doctors say, or what you might think has compromised your ability to conceive. It doesn't matter how old you are or how long you've waited. As long as you believe, God will make it happen.

Trust His timing. Move by faith, not by sight. God's promise to Sarah is alive today, a timeless assurance of hope and blessing for every expecting mom.

Prayer

Heavenly Father,

Thank you Lord for your promise and the precious gift of bearing children. I declare that our womb is blessed by your hand. I stand firm on every word you have spoken concerning our children, and just as you fulfilled your promise to Sarah, I trust in your perfect timing.

Thank you for being a faithful God through all generations, unchanging, steadfast, and true. I lift up every woman who is waiting patiently on your promise to bear children. May you hold them close, wipe away their tears, strengthen their hearts, and perform miracles in their lives.

I surrender their anxieties and fears into your gracious hands and help them choose to embrace your joy instead. Fill them with your peace and grant them the patience to wait on you faithfully.

Thank you for your divine timing, and for the testimony you are shaping through them. I serve a God who always keeps His promises.

In Jesus' name. Amen.

Reflections of Grace

- ✝ What promises are you trusting God to fulfill in your life or in the lives of your children?

- ✝ How do you usually respond when God's timing feels slower, or different, than what you had hoped for?

✝ In what ways might God be using this season of waiting to grow your patience and strengthen your faith as a mother?

_____

_____

_____

_____

_____

_____

_____

_____

_____

_____

_____

_____

_____

_____

_____

_____

_____

_____

_____

_____

_____

CHAPTER
THREE

Blessed Among Women: The Gift of New Life

> 📖 **Luke 1:42**
>
> *Elizabeth spoke: "Blessed are you among women, and blessed is the child you will bear!"*

While pregnancy is often a joyful and eagerly awaited time, for some women it can bring unexpected trials, whether it's facing pregnancy out of wedlock, feeling abandoned by the baby's father, or other difficult circumstances. These situations can bring uncertainty and make the journey ahead feel defeated.

Even when life seems unfair and things feel like they've taken a wrong turn, I want to remind you of this powerful truth: no matter what you're going through, you and your child are truly blessed. This may be hard to grasp right now, but it is real and it is true.

As you walk this long road, sometimes feeling alone, I want you to know that the Lord is close beside you. He has allowed this journey for a purpose, and you never know how things might change for the better down the line. I have heard countless stories of women who faced heartbreak and despair in similar situations but emerged stronger, with renewed hope and determination.

Motherhood brings its tests and milestones, but in those tough moments, I pray you remember: you are blessed, and so is your baby. I pray you hold tightly to this truth as you learn to love and provide for your child.

Prayer

Heavenly Father,

Your daughters stand at a crossroads feeling alone on this new journey of motherhood. Some are unsure if they are ready for what lies ahead. But today, I choose to meditate on your word and believe that, regardless of their circumstances, they are blessed. Thank you for this assurance. Thank you for guiding every step of this new chapter and for providing all they need. Thank You for sending helpers to strengthen and support them. Thank you for this very moment, this new beginning, when you saw fit for them to become a mom despite their doubts. Thank you for the precious gift of new life.

In Jesus' name, Amen.

Reflections of Grace

✝ In what ways do you recognize motherhood as a blessing, even on the most challenging days?

✝ What are the small, everyday moments that remind you of the precious gift your children are to you?

✝ When struggles arise, how can you shift your focus to see God's hand at work and rediscover the blessing in this season of motherhood?

_____

_____

_____

_____

_____

_____

_____

_____

_____

_____

_____

_____

_____

_____

_____

_____

_____

_____

CHAPTER
FOUR

The Labor of Love

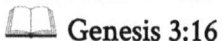 **Genesis 3:16**

"To the woman he said, 'I will greatly multiply your pain in childbearing; in pain you shall bring forth children. Your desire shall be for your husband, and he shall rule over you."

Before becoming a mother myself, I had heard about women's labor experiences: the pain, the long hours, and the recovery. Though those stories sounded intimidating, and despite my own fear of pain, I still longed for motherhood. What struck me most was that the very women who shared their stories went on to have more children, as if the pain became only a faint memory. I thought, if they can do it, so can I.

But when my moment came, the reality of labor was unlike anything I had ever imagined. The pain was excruciating, truly beyond description. This was not God's original intent for us; rather, it is a consequence of sin entering the world, affecting not only the physical pain of childbirth but also the emotional struggles of motherhood and even the dynamics between men and women.

I was deeply grateful for the blessing of modern medicine, especially the epidural. I honestly don't think I could have endured eight hours of labor before being rushed into an emergency C-section without it. I admire and applaud every mother who gives birth without medication!

Though childbirth is painful, it is also the pathway through which we meet our precious children. And I know every mother, myself included, would walk that road again for the sake of our little ones.

Prayer

Heavenly Father,

We acknowledge that the pain of childbirth is a result of sin's entrance into the world. Yet, even in the discomfort, we thank you for the experience. Remind us that beyond the suffering lies your promise of redemption: healing our hearts, restoring relationships, and removing all pain.

In Jesus' name, Amen.

Reflections of Grace

✝ In your journey as a mother, how have you experienced both the deep joys and the difficult hardships that come with this calling?

✝ How do the emotional, physical, and spiritual challenges of motherhood reflect the truth of this verse?

✝ When weariness or frustration sets in, what helps you remember that you are never alone in your struggles and that God is present with you?

_____

_____

_____

_____

_____

_____

_____

_____

_____

_____

_____

_____

_____

_____

_____

_____

_____

_____

CHAPTER
FIVE

The Song of Surrender

> 📖 Luke 1: 46-48
>
> *"And Mary said: My soul glorifies the Lord and my spirit rejoices in God my Savior, for He has been mindful of the humble state of his servant. From now on all generations will call me blessed."*

Mary was betrothed to Joseph, preparing for marriage, when the angel Gabriel appeared with a message that would change her life forever: she would conceive and give birth to Jesus, the Son of God. At that moment, Mary responded with a song of surrender. She understood the consequences of her situation, an unmarried woman pregnant in a society governed by strict moral codes, but she still chose to trust God and submit to His will.

Back then, such a pregnancy could bring shame, rejection, and even danger. Yet Mary's faith never wavered. And God, in His divine wisdom, reassured Joseph, explaining that this child was conceived by the Holy Spirit and part of His perfect plan. What courage and trust

Mary displayed! Her response is a model for us as mothers: to surrender fully to God's timing and plan, trusting Him even when the path seems uncertain or difficult.

I remember the moment I discovered I was pregnant. Tears of joy filled my eyes as I rejoiced that this long-awaited moment had finally arrived. My husband's response was one of awe and acknowledgment of God's faithfulness. For many mothers, the news of a pregnancy is met with joy and gratitude, but we know that circumstances can sometimes bring fear or uncertainty.

What if we approached the discovery of pregnancy like Mary, seeing it as an invitation to surrender, to trust God, and to believe that He will work all things for our good? No matter the unknowns, God is mindful of us and will guide us every step of the way.

Prayer

Heavenly Father,

Thank you for the gift of life and the blessing of pregnancy. Like Mary, help us surrender fully to your will, trusting that you are at work even in uncertainty. Comfort every mother facing the unknown, fill their heart with peace, and remind them that you are mindful of them and their child.

In Jesus' name, Amen.

Reflections of Grace

✝ In what practical ways can you honor and glorify God through your words, actions, and attitude as a mother this week?

✝ What would it look like for your soul to truly magnify the Lord, even in the midst of everyday moments, folding laundry, preparing meals, or tucking your little ones into bed?

_____

_____

_____

_____

_____

_____

_____

_____

_____

_____

_____

_____

_____

_____

_____

_____

CHAPTER
SIX

Inheritance of the Lord

📖 **Psalm 127: 3-5**

"Children are a heritage from the Lord, offspring a reward from him. Like arrows in the hands of a warrior are children born in one's youth. Blessed is the man whose quiver is full of them."

Children are a heritage, a gift, and a precious blessing from the Lord. They are also a reflection of our honor and purpose in this world.

As a proud mother of one, it fills me with indescribable joy to speak about my son. Watching him grow, and witnessing how God is shaping and molding his life, gives me a deep sense of purpose and renewed grit. Knowing that God has entrusted his life into the care of my husband and I is both humbling and empowering. It influences every choice we make.

Giving up is no longer an option, because I have the privilege of playing a part in the unfolding of his God-given purpose.

Parenting is not something to be taken lightly. Children are not merely the result of biology, as the world might suggest, they are our spiritual legacy.

Prayer

Heavenly Father,

Thank you for the gift of our children. Truly, they are an inheritance from you. Help us to see them as you do: full of value, purpose, and potential. Lead us as we raise them, and guide our hearts and hands with your wisdom and love.

In Jesus' name, Amen.

Reflections of Grace

✠ How might seeing your children as a precious gift from God transform the way you approach the difficult moments of motherhood?

✠ In what ways can you show gratitude to God for the privilege of raising the children He has entrusted to you, even on the hardest days?

_____

_____

CHAPTER
SEVEN

Created with Purpose: A God-Known Identity

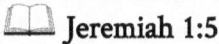 **Jeremiah 1:5**

"Before I formed you in the womb I knew you, before you were born I set you apart; I appointed you as a prophet to the nations."

How many of you moms truly believe your child was created with a divine purpose? Psalms 139 is one of my favorite passages because it reveals how deeply God knows us, even before we existed as a thought in our parents' minds or were conceived in the womb. It reminds us that God's presence surrounds us always, that our days are ordained by Him, and that we are fearfully and wonderfully made. Jeremiah 1:5 echoes this truth, emphasizing our unique identity and mission in the world. We are set apart, appointed for a purpose greater than ourselves.

As mothers, while we are the vessels God uses to bring our children into this world, our children ultimately belong to Him. Each one carries a powerful destiny and a purpose beyond our understanding. God has placed a divine mandate on their lives to impact the world for His glory.

Our role as mothers is to pray without ceasing, asking God to reveal His plan for our children's lives so we can nurture their gifts and guide them on the right path. In a world filled with problems and distractions that seek to derail them, only through prayer and intercession can our children fulfill their God-given destiny.

We have a sacred mission to remain at Jesus' feet on behalf of our children, to keep them hidden under the shadow of the cross, growing as Disciples of Christ, and shining His light boldly in the darkness. While achievements like degrees and worldly success are worthy of celebration, they pale in comparison to a life fully surrendered to God's purpose. Without Him, those accomplishments ultimately mean little to nothing.

May we, as mothers, never abandon our post, standing in the gap, guiding, and counseling our children with the Word of Life.

Prayer

Heavenly Father,

Thank you for reminding us that the children you have entrusted to us already have a plan over their lives designed by you. You have called them for a divine purpose to impact nations. We ask for your wisdom to raise them in your likeness, that they may follow you all their days. We rebuke every attack from the enemy that seeks to cause them to forfeit their destiny. We declare that our children will fulfill the calling you have placed on their lives. Hide them securely under your wings, and let your angels always surround and protect them. Thank you for setting them apart for such a time as this.

In Jesus' name, Amen.

Reflections of Grace

✝ How comforting is it to realize that God knew and lovingly designed your children long before you ever held them in your arms?

✝ What does this truth reveal about the incredible value and unique identity your child has in God's eyes?

✝ How might remembering that your children ultimately belong to Him help you let go of fear, surrender control, and trust His perfect plan more fully?

_____

_____

_____

_____

_____

_____

_____

_____

CHAPTER
EIGHT

A Dwelling Filled with Grace

 **Psalm 128:3**

"Your wife will be like a fruitful vine within your house;
your children will be like olive shoots around your table.

For those of us who are wives, and for those who long to be, this verse wonderfully illustrates the effects of a good wife and mother. She brings life, growth, and blessing into the home. She embodies abundance, productivity, and nurturing influence. Just as a vine grows strong and spreads wide, a mother plays a vital role in nurturing her family and cultivating a flourishing home. Through her presence, prayers, love, and care, she becomes a source of spiritual and emotional fruit for her children.

Our children, compared to olive shoots, reflect vitality and growth, nurtured by our care. For us mothers, the greatest reward is seeing our children thrive in a safe and loving environment. Beyond this, a good wife and mother shapes the family dynamic, fostering closeness, unity, and harmony.

As a wife and mother, being a fruitful vine allows our families to thrive, making both us and our children sources of joy for our husbands. Psalm 128:3 reminds mothers that their sacrifices and devotion are seen by God. He has designed us to be a source of fruitfulness, with our children serving as a living testimony of His blessing. This verse captures the honor and sacred calling of motherhood, a reminder that raising children and building a Godly home is both precious and divinely celebrated.

Prayer

Heavenly Father,

Thank you for calling us fruitful vines, capable of sowing hope, joy, and prosperity in our homes. Thank you for revealing that these fruits can extend to our children and family, placing us at the heart of togetherness in our households. We declare and decree that this shall be our portion.

In Jesus' name, Amen.

Reflections of Grace

✟ What kind of spiritual fruit do you long to see growing in your life as a mother, such as patience, joy, or faithfulness?

✟ How are you actively nurturing your relationship with God so that you can pour His love and wisdom into your family?

✝ Are there habits, distractions, or influences that may be draining your spiritual strength? How can you prune them away to create space for deeper growth and fruitfulness?

_____

_____

_____

_____

_____

_____

_____

_____

_____

_____

_____

_____

_____

_____

_____

_____

_____

_____

_____

_____

_____

CHAPTER

NINE

Restoring Hope: The Gift of a Happy Home

> 📖 **Psalm 113:9**
>
> *"He settles the childless woman in her home as a happy mother of children. Praise the Lord."*

I have a lively toddler son who fills our home with excitement and laughter every day. Often, I pause quietly and thank God in my heart for this incredible blessing. The blessing of waking up surrounded by my loving husband and handsome boy. The blessing of picking up toys countless times a day, the blessing of chasing after my son during bath time, the blessing of peaceful afternoon naps and refreshing walks, the blessing of warm hugs and sweet kisses, the blessing of watching him grow strong and healthy.

Growing up, I longed deeply to become a mother one day. That longing only grew stronger as the years passed. For a while, it felt distant and out of reach, but now I'm living one of my most heartfelt answered prayers. Can any other moms relate? Praise be to the Most High God for hearing those silent, tearful prayers. He placed me in a home with a child I prayed and hoped for. He has given me more than I could ever imagine. Who else but Him could have done that for me?

As you reflect on this Bible verse this week, I encourage you to pause in the midst of your busy days and lift a praise to God for the precious gift of motherhood and family. It's easy to take these moments for granted, caught up in the day-to-day rush. But every second we spend with our children and loved ones is an opportunity to recognize just how blessed we truly are. Many of us are living testimonies of God's unfailing goodness. Let us never forget this truth, and let us joyfully share how the Lord has made us happy mothers in our homes. Praise the Lord!

Prayer

Heavenly Father,

We cannot thank you enough for the incredible gift of motherhood, for surrounding us with wonderful children and loving families. May we never forget your graciousness in blessing our lives so abundantly. Help us always to be mindful and grateful as we raise your sons and daughters for your glory. Thank you for allowing our wombs to bear fruit and for establishing us as joyful mothers in our homes. May our mouths never cease to praise you.

In Jesus' name, Amen.

Reflections of Grace

✝ How can you intentionally show gratitude for the privilege of raising the children He has placed in your care?

✝ What unique qualities or special moments with each of your children can you thank God for this week?

_____

_____

_____

_____

_____

_____

_____

_____

_____

_____

_____

_____

_____

_____

_____

_____

_____

CHAPTER
TEN

Training for a Lifetime

 Proverbs 22:6

"Train up a child in the way he should go, and when he is old, he will not depart from it."

Do you ever look at the world and feel a pang of worry for your children's future? Their walk with the Lord? The choices they will face as they grow into adulthood? When they're young, it feels easier to shield and guide them. But we know there will come a day when they must take ownership of their lives.

As mothers, our instinct is to protect, to keep them safe from harm and danger. Yet, we can only do this for so long. They will go to school, meet people from all walks of life, and make friends who may not share their faith. That's why this Bible verse is so powerful: "Train up a child in the way he should go, and when he is old, he will not depart from it."

My husband and I began praying for our son before he even entered this world, dedicating him to the Lord and covering his future in prayer. When he was born, we introduced him to God's Word early. You too, can train your children according to their age, understanding, and stage of development.

I'm no expert, and I don't claim to have it all figured out. But here are a few things I've found helpful, both in my own home and from watching other parents:

- **Establish an atmosphere of prayer.** Let prayer be as natural as conversation in your home. There are wonderful children's prayer books to help guide them.

- **Spend time in God's Word together**. Daily family devotions don't have to be long, but they should be consistent.

- **Lead by example**. Children are keen observers, they will imitate what they see more than what they hear.

- **Incorporate praise and worship.** Singing together can plant truth deep in their hearts.

- **Connect with a faith community.** Being part of a home church or fellowship where they are surrounded by other believers is invaluable.

- **Equip them for spiritual warfare.** Teach them how to recognize and stand against the enemy's schemes.

- **Help them remember/know their worth.** Speak daily affirmations grounded in scripture over them, declaring their identity in Christ.

It all starts at home. If we lay a strong, Godly foundation, those truths will go with them into the world. And once we've done our part, we can rest in the assurance that God will handle the rest.

Prayer

Heavenly Father,

Thank you for the incredible privilege and responsibility of leading our children to you. We acknowledge that we cannot do this without your wisdom, guidance, and grace. Teach us to raise our children to be faithful disciples in a world that's turning away from you. We declare and decree that our children will follow you all the days of their lives.

In Jesus' name, Amen.

Reflections of Grace

✝ What spiritual groundwork are you building in your home today?

✝ In what practical, everyday ways are you introducing your children to God's Word and His presence?

✝ Are there areas of your parenting where you sense God calling you to be more intentional in planting seeds of faith that will grow for years to come?

_____

_____

_____

_____

_____

_____

_____

_____

_____

_____

_____

_____

_____

_____

_____

_____

_____

_____

_____

_____

CHAPTER

ELEVEN

A Tradition of Faith

> 📖 **Psalm 78:4**
>
> *"We will not hide them from their descendants; we will tell the next generation the praiseworthy deeds of the Lord, His power, and the wonders He has done."*

I get genuinely excited whenever I have the chance to share a testimony about what God has done in my life. Whether it's in a small setting or before a whole congregation, speaking of God's mighty works fills me with joy, knowing it can strengthen and encourage others. But what if we took that same approach with our own children? Imagine the impact of sitting down with them and sharing how our lives are living testimonies of God's power.

Each of us has faced troubles that we know we couldn't have overcome without God showing up. Some of us are walking miracles. Personally, I've had encounters where the Lord came to my rescue, moments when I should have died, not once but twice, and yet God said, "Not today."

Part of raising Godly children is sharing these personal experiences with them. Sure, they can hear stories at church or from others, but there's something uniquely powerful about hearing life-changing testimonies from their parents. I know this because I still vividly remember my grandmother's stories about overcoming witchcraft and battling evil spirits while raising my mother and her siblings. I also recall moments when my mother should have died, but through the power of prayer, God hindered every plan of the enemy.

Take time to ensure your children know that we serve a powerful God, the one and only Jesus Christ. Meet them where they are, and the seeds you plant will bear fruit for years to come.

Prayer

Heavenly Father,

You have been so good to me. Your love has delivered me from situations that should have claimed my life. That I am still here today is living proof of your unstoppable power, grace, and mercy. Help me to boldly share how you have rescued me, not only with others but especially with my children, so that your name will be praised in my family, long after I am gone.

In Jesus' name, Amen.

Reflections of Grace

✝ What personal stories or testimonies from your life can you share to help your children recognize God's hand at work?

✝ How can you create meaningful and memorable moments that bring God's Word to life for your family?

_____

_____

_____

_____

_____

_____

_____

_____

_____

_____

_____

_____

_____

_____

_____

_____

_____

_____

_____

_____

_____

CHAPTER
TWELVE

Guided by Wisdom:
The Legacy of Loving Discipline

📖 **Proverbs 1:8-9**

"Listen, my son, to your father's instruction and do not forsake your mother's teaching. They are a garland to grace your head and a chain to adorn your neck."

Growing up, I didn't always understand my parents' discipline or the reasons behind their rules. To me, it just felt like a list of restrictions, things I wasn't allowed to do or be part of. But looking back now, I realize that although my parents didn't always know how to explain the reasons behind their guidance, their love was evident. More importantly, their discipline protected me from vulnerability to harmful influences.

For instance, my siblings and I were never allowed to have sleepovers at friends' homes. At the time, we thought it would be fun to spend the night, but now, hearing heartbreaking stories of abuse and trauma, I'm deeply grateful for the protection that boundary provided.

I don't believe we always need to explain every reason behind our decisions to our children, but it's crucial they understand one thing clearly: our guidance comes from a place of love. Love should be the driving force behind our discipline, and our children should feel secure knowing we have their best interest at heart.

In the same way God calls us to follow His commands to avoid the traps of the enemy, as mothers, we are called to teach and instill wisdom in our children through loving discipline. The ways we guide and correct our children serve as a protective shield over their lives.

Prayer

Heavenly Father,

This journey of parenting and motherhood is not easy. Many days we wonder if we're doing right by our children. Please guide us to balance love and discipline so they may grow to honor you and treat others with kindness. When our patience is tested, give us strength to remain calm and loving. We thank you for being with us as we learn to love and correct our children the same way you lovingly guide us.

In Jesus' name, Amen.

Reflections of Grace

✝ How does this verse inspire you to embrace both the spiritual responsibility and your role as a mother and teacher to your children?

✝ As you reflect on your own journey, what wisdom or life lessons from your parents, mentors, or spiritual influences can you intentionally pass down to help your children grow in their walk with the Lord?

✝ In guiding and shaping their hearts, how can you strike a balance between correction and encouragement, so that your words and actions nurture them with grace and love rather than pressure or fear?

CHAPTER
THIRTEEN

Guarding the Hearts of Our Children

 Colossians 3:21

"Fathers, do not provoke your children, lest they become discouraged."

Y ou might be wondering why I chose to base a chapter on a Bible verse addressed to fathers. The answer is simple: parenting requires both a mother and a father. While fathers are often seen as the primary disciplinarians, mothers are called to the same responsibility. It's no coincidence that this chapter follows the previous one on loving discipline.

I grew up in a Haitian household, where discipline played a significant role in how my siblings and I were raised. The Bible mentions discipline repeatedly, and I wholeheartedly encourage it, but it must never be used in a way that consistently provokes, frustrates, or discourages our children. Discipline should be fair, balanced, and tempered with compassion.

As mothers, we are called to nurture our children, guiding them to grow in faith, character, and confidence. We must be careful not to push them toward discouragement, resentment, or hopelessness. Will we always get it right? No. Motherhood and parenting in general is a learning journey. Since we are all flawed, mistakes are inevitable.

But there is power in acknowledging our mistakes and asking our children for forgiveness when we have wronged them. Doing so fosters trust and helps them understand that just as they need grace when they mess up, we do too. Furthermore, it illustrates our reliance on God's grace, a gift we do not deserve.

Prayer

Heavenly Father,

Thank you for reminding us that our role is to build our children up, not tear them down. Help us lead with love, and discipline with care. And when we fall short and cause them pain, give us the courage to admit our mistakes, so our children can thrive, remain encouraged, and grow closer to you.

In Jesus' name, Amen.

Reflections of Grace

✝ How do your words and actions shape the hearts of your children, either building them up or unintentionally tearing them down?

✞ When correction or discipline is needed, how can you make sure it flows from love and a desire to guide, rather than from frustration or anger?

✞ Think about times when you've sensed discouragement in your child's heart. How can you respond in those moments with grace, encouragement, and remind them of their worth in God's eyes?

_____

_____

_____

_____

_____

_____

_____

_____

_____

_____

_____

_____

_____

_____

_____

_____

CHAPTER
FOURTEEN

Resting in God's Gentle Embrace

 Isaiah 66:13

"As one whom his mother comforts, so I will comfort you; you shall be comforted in Jerusalem."

This Bible verse truly warms my heart and confirms the profound comfort we mothers provide to our children. It's a gift God has uniquely placed within us. I've learned to be more intentional about being fully present when my son comes to me for comfort in his pain, cherishing those moments of embrace. God has designed us to be a safe refuge for our little ones. What moves me even more is that God Himself compares the comfort we offer our children to the comfort we find in Him.

There's a divine reason why we can calm our children in the midst of tantrums, no matter how overwhelmed they are by their emotions. Why when they're sick, they long to be held. Why when fear grips them, they run into our arms. Mothers, never underestimate your value. The comfort you give your children is a reflection of the same peace that can only be found in Jesus Christ.

So, I encourage you to be intentional: to be truly present when your child needs that extra hug, that gentle kiss, or simply more time.

Prayer

Heavenly Father,

What a precious privilege it is to know that you comfort us as we comfort our children. Help us never to take this sacred task lightly. Fill our hearts and souls so we can pour love and peace into our children when they need it most. When life feels overthrowing and it's hard to pause, remind us of your word, so we may stop and give our children the love and attention they need.

In Jesus' name. Amen.

Reflections of Grace

✝ How does it encourage your heart to know that God's comfort toward you is just as tender, personal, and intimate as the way you lovingly comfort your own children?

✝ When was the last time you paused and allowed yourself to fully rest in His arms, letting go of your worries and trusting Him to carry every burden?

✝ In this season of life and motherhood, where do you most
   need to experience God's comforting presence?

_____

_____

_____

_____

_____

_____

_____

_____

_____

_____

_____

_____

_____

_____

_____

_____

_____

_____

_____

_____

CHAPTER
FIFTEEN

Strength and Dignity:
The Woman of Noble Character

📖 **Proverbs 31: 25-28**

"Strength and dignity are her clothing, and she laughs at the time to come. She opens her mouth with wisdom, and the teaching of kindness is on her tongue. She looks well to the ways of her household and does not eat the bread of idleness. Her children rise up and call her blessed; her husband also, and he praises her."

A s mothers, we set the atmosphere in our homes.

The way we carry ourselves and the words we speak hold tremendous influence over our families. I'll be the first to admit, this isn't always easy. We wear many hats: wife, mother, sister, daughter, granddaughter, professional, and more. With so many expectations placed upon us, some days can feel completely rough.

Yet, our home is our first ministry.

While it's important to show up with grace and strength in our roles outside the home, we cannot do so at the expense of our own household. Our families need us present: emotionally, spiritually, and mentally. But for that to happen, we must first take care of ourselves. That means checking in with our well-being and creating space to rest, recharge, and reconnect.

I've come to learn that even small acts of self-care: a manicure, a massage, a quiet moment in prayer, or simply getting our hair done can help us reset. These things aren't luxuries; they are tools that allow us to feel restored so we can pour into others from a place of fullness, not depletion.

On the days when it's hard to show up for ourselves or for those we love, we can lean on the Word of God for strength. It is our anchor, our source of truth and motivation.

I pray that the Lord gives us grace to speak life, love, and wisdom into our homes. May our words be gentle and kind, and our hearts tender and strong. We can only live this out fully through the power of Jesus Christ.

Prayer

Heavenly Father,

I come before you in my brokenness. Please guard the words that come from my mouth. Help me be a source of love and kindness to my husband and my children. Wake me each day with a sound, renewed mind, ready to walk in my purpose, especially within my own home. Teach me how to care for my family with wisdom and grace. Let my household rise and call me blessed, not for my perfection, but for the love and faith I pour into them. Make me the mother and wife you've created me to be.

In Jesus' name. Amen.

Reflections of Grace

✝ What does it mean for you, in this season of motherhood, to be "clothed with strength and dignity"? How does living in that truth shape the way you navigate challenges and care for your family?

✝ What would it look like for your children to "rise up and call you blessed," not only through their words, but through the way they live, the choices they make, and the values they carry into the world?

_____

_____

_____

_____

_____

_____

_____

_____

CHAPTER
SIXTEEN

Walking in Trust

 Psalm 37:5

"Commit your way to the Lord; trust in Him and He will act."

So far, we've explored various topics around pregnancy, motherhood, and wifehood. I want to pause and ask you: what are your personal goals and aspirations? What do you feel God is calling you to do beyond these roles?

In my own journey as a wife and mother of one, I often find it challenging to carve out time to reflect on my life's goals. Working nights only makes it harder to focus on anything beyond the immediate demands of daily life. We pour so much into raising children, supporting our spouses, and caring for others that we sometimes neglect nurturing our own purpose.

This week, I encourage you to reflect: what is one accomplishment you are truly proud of? Where do you see yourself in the years ahead? Do you feel you are walking in the fullness of God's plan for your life? If not, don't give up on your dreams.

Writing has always been a deep desire of my heart. And now, at age 36, the Lord pressed me to finally write this devotional for women like me who are trying to balance it all. God's timing is perfect, and it's never too late to pursue your calling. Striving to be the best woman you can be can also inspire your children to reach their own potential.

As you reflect this week, take time to write down the goals God has placed in your heart. Bring them to Him in prayer, commit your way to the Lord, trust in His timing, and watch Him make it happen.

Prayer

Heavenly Father,

There is so much more to us than the roles and titles we navigate each day. Just as we nurture the hopes of those around us, help us find the strength to fulfill our God-given purpose and excel in our gifts. Reignite the fire within us to pursue our goals, and help us overcome every obstacle that comes our way. We thank you Lord for your guidance, for we place our trust in you.

In Jesus' name. Amen.

Reflections of Grace

✝ When you encounter seasons of uncertainty or fear, what intentional steps can you take to demonstrate your trust by fully committing your ways to God?

✝ Are there dreams, expectations, or carefully laid plans you've been holding onto that He may be inviting you to surrender into His hands?

_____

_____

_____

_____

_____

_____

_____

_____

_____

_____

_____

_____

_____

_____

_____

CHAPTER
SEVENTEEN

When Grace Meets Weakness

 2 Corinthians 12:9

"My grace is sufficient for you, for my power is made perfect in weakness."

Some days, I wake up feeling empowered, ready to take on anything the day throws my way. Other days, I have to push myself just to get out of bed. I feel drained, depleted, and weary. On those mornings, I don't want to be a mom, a wife, or an employee. I just long for a moment where I can simply be me.

If I'm being completely honest, there are weeks when it feels like everything that could go wrong... does. I find myself wondering, how much more can I take? And I know I'm not the only one who has felt that way. At the end of the day, we're human. We can only carry so much before our cups run dry. But we must guard our hearts from slipping into despair and depression.

When my strength is gone, I'm grateful for a God whose strength never runs out. In those low moments, praise and worship lift my spirit first, followed by prayer, even if it's just a silent whisper to the Lord. Stepping outside for a quiet afternoon walk, breathing in fresh air, and soaking in the beauty of nature without a to-do list hovering over my mind brings me back to life.

As mothers, we must give ourselves permission to acknowledge these feelings and discover the things that refill our cups. God's grace meets us in our weakness, gently restoring our drive and renewing our hope.

Prayer

Heavenly Father

Thank you for being our strength when we are weak, and for reminding us that your grace is enough. Restore our energy when it fades, and keep our hearts from staying in low places.

Thank you for carrying us through even the most trying days.

In Jesus' name. Amen.

Reflections of Grace

✝ How can you embrace and even rejoice in your weaknesses, recognizing them as opportunities to depend on Jesus more deeply each day?

✝ Reflect on a recent moment when you felt like giving up. How did God's strength sustain you in that situation? In what ways did that experience deepen your trust and strengthen your faith?

CHAPTER
EIGHTEEN

Anchored in Hope

> 📖 **Psalm 31:24**
>
> *"Be strong and take heart, all you who hope in the Lord."*

Have you ever felt yourself teetering on the edge of a meltdown, so close to desperation that you had to whisper to yourself, "I have to be strong"? But what does being strong really mean to you?

Does it mean ignoring the fact that you might need help, or reassurance? While it's true that encouraging ourselves can help us push through the day-to-day, we must be careful not to numb ourselves in the process.

You are still a strong mom if you take five minutes in the bathroom without your little one trailing behind. Sometimes when I'm getting ready for work, I have to shower with the bathroom door open; otherwise, my son will scream the whole time. You are still a strong mom if you want to enjoy a warm shower without feeling rushed. You are still a strong mom if you need a burden lifted from your shoulders.

I hope that came through clearly: the pressure to "be strong" for our families can quietly lead to exhaustion if we're not careful.

In this verse, "strong" isn't about sheer physical might, it's an invitation from our Lord to stand firm even when life feels uncertain or frightening. It's not about self-reliance alone but about leaning fully on God's presence, promises, and faithfulness.

Prayer

Heavenly Father,

Thank you that when our hope is in you, we don't have to rely on our own strength or pretend we have it all together. Thank you for meeting us in our vulnerable moments and for calling us into a place where we seek you first. We're grateful that in every season, we can trust in you.

In Jesus' name. Amen.

Reflections of Grace

✝ What does it truly mean to "take heart" when you feel weary, overwhelmed, or unsure of what lies ahead?

✝ How can you intentionally place your hope in the Lord, trusting His plan instead of leaning on your own strength or expectations?

✝ As you reflect on past seasons of motherhood, how have you experienced God's sustaining power? How can those moments of His faithfulness inspire and encourage you in the week ahead?

_____

_____

_____

_____

_____

_____

_____

_____

_____

_____

_____

_____

_____

_____

_____

_____

_____

_____

_____

_____

CHAPTER
NINETEEN

His Yoke, Our Freedom

📖 **Matthew 11: 28**

"Come to me, all you who are weary and burdened, and I will give you rest."

fter I had my son, the postpartum season was one of the most challenging times of my life. I was healing from a C-section, struggling through breastfeeding difficulties, and learning how to care for this precious baby, with barely any outside help. In those early days, it was just God, my husband, and our son.

Uncertainty loomed over everything. We wondered if we were doing the right things, fought through countless sleepless nights, and spent hours soothing our baby through painful gas episodes. For a while, I thought I was managing well, until the crying spells started. Without realizing it, I had slipped into postpartum depression.

It was my husband who gently brought it to my attention. Alongside his prayers, he encouraged me to talk to a Christian counselor. I was weary and burdened, but through prayer and those counseling sessions, God reminded me of something profound: He had given me this child because He knew I had what it takes to care for him. He reassured me that the Holy Spirit living in me would guide me through every milestone of my son's life.

God even led me to resources and books that helped me grow as a mother. Slowly, I reached a place where I could sleep peacefully at night without anxiously watching my baby breathe, terrified something might happen.

That fear had deep roots. When my baby was born, he didn't cry right away, the umbilical cord was wrapped around his neck. The operating room went silent. I remember asking over and over, "Why isn't my baby crying?" By the grace of God, he was okay, but that moment left a deep trauma in me. It wasn't until I spoke with the counselor that I realized my constant fear was rooted in believing my baby might die. Surrendering that fear to God finally brought me peace.

So, I ask you: what in your motherhood journey has left you weary and burdened? Do you believe you could find true rest if you surrendered those fears fully to God? Would you be willing to seek help, spiritual and professional, if you needed it?

For me, prayer and speaking with a Christian counselor, whom God used as a vessel to speak life into me, changed everything.

Prayer

Heavenly Father,

We bring before you every worry and burden, knowing only you can help us overcome them. We surrender our minds and thoughts to you. Let your Holy Spirit take control and replace every lie with your truth. Thank you for working in and through us. Thank you for the gift of rest.

In Jesus' name. Amen.

Reflections of Grace

✝ Which aspects of motherhood feel the heaviest for you in this season, and how can you intentionally lay those burdens at the feet of Jesus?

✝ What lies, expectations, or pressures are you holding onto that God is inviting you to release, so you can experience the deep, soul-refreshing rest He promises?

_____

_____

_____

_____

_____

_____

_____

CHAPTER
TWENTY

Held by His Presence

 **Psalm 46:5**

"God is within her, she will not fall; God will help her at break of day."

How we start our day matters more than we often realize. The first moments of the morning can set the tone for how we handle the rest of the day, including the unexpected dilemmas that may arise.

One of the most powerful habits we can form is beginning each day with prayer. It doesn't have to be long or eloquent. A simple moment to thank God for His protection during the night, to acknowledge His presence in our lives, and to surrender the day to Him can make all the difference.

Psalm 46:5 reminds us that God is within us, and because of His constant presence, we will not fall into temptation, out of character, or into anything that draws us away from Him. He promises to help us, not halfway through the day, not after we've tried everything on our own, but at break of day. That means His help is available right from the start, if we're willing to invite Him in.

God recently gave me the revelation that this promise isn't just something to believe, it's something we must claim each morning. Life comes with unexpected twists and turns, but when we align ourselves with His Word at the beginning of the day, we activate that promise and position ourselves to overcome.

We already have the tools we need to thrive in every area of life, and the Word of God is our greatest weapon. Prayer is one way we access its power. When we begin our day in His presence, we are strengthened to face anything.

Prayer

Heavenly Father,

Thank you for the promise that because you live within us, we will not fall. Thank you for being our help from the very start of the day. Teach us to begin each morning with gratitude, surrender, and trust. Help us to claim this promise daily and walk in the confidence that, with you, failure is not our portion.

In Jesus' name, Amen.

Reflections of Grace

✝ In what areas of your life or motherhood do you need the gentle reminder that you will not fall because God is holding you steady?

✝ What daily rhythms can you create to stay closely connected to Him so that His peace and strength shape your words, actions, and decisions?

✝ How can you begin each day with a heart of trust, confident that God is already ahead of you, ready to guide and help you?

_____

_____

_____

_____

_____

_____

_____

_____

_____

_____

_____

_____

CHAPTER
TWENTY-ONE
Serving with Resolve

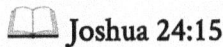 Joshua 24:15

"But as for me and my household, we will serve the Lord."

What does it truly mean to serve the Lord?

We often hear this verse quoted, but do we really grasp its depth? Originally, it was a call to the Israelites to choose between serving false gods or the one true Living God. Today, it calls each of us to make a deliberate decision to serve Jesus Christ.

While this is a wonderful decision to embrace personally and to nurture in our children, it requires intentionality and a personal commitment to fully follow God. There are days when I'm so exhausted that finding the time and energy to pray with my son feels like a challenge. By the time he's ready for bed, I'm ready to collapse myself. Yet, even on those nights, I know how important it is to cover him in prayer. If I don't have the strength to kneel beside his bed, I try to whisper prayers over him as he drifts off to sleep in my arms.

Serving the Lord calls for persistence, a willingness to push past fatigue and inconvenience, because these small, faithful moments matter more than we realize.

Serving the Lord is more than attending church weekly or participating in religious activities; it is a lifestyle and a posture of the heart that seeks to reflect God's character and follow His will in all things.

May we no longer recite this verse without embracing the intentional faith it demands. May our actions align with our words, and may we nurture these values in our children, inspiring future generations to serve faithfully.

Prayer

Heavenly Father,

Thank you for giving us the ability to choose to serve you and walk in your ways. Help us Lord to remain fully committed to this decision each day and to be living examples of what it truly means to serve you to our children. May we honor only you, the true Living God, all the days of our lives.

In Jesus' name, Amen.

Reflections of Grace

✝ What does it mean for you, personally, to boldly declare that your home will serve the Lord?

✝ In what areas of your family life do you find it most challenging to stay faithful to this commitment?

✝ How can you intentionally model a life of service to God, through your actions, words, and daily decisions, so your children can see His love and truth lived out in you?

_____

_____

_____

_____

_____

_____

_____

_____

_____

_____

_____

_____

_____

_____

_____

_____

_____

_____

CHAPTER
TWENTY-TWO

Her Value is Beyond Rubies

> 📖 **Proverbs 31:10-12**
>
> *"A wife of noble character who can find? She is worth far more than rubies. Her husband has full confidence in her and lacks nothing of value."*

Whether you are a mother who is also a wife, or a mother who aspires to be a wife one day, this verse speaks directly to you. Motherhood can absorb so much of our energy and attention that, if we're not careful, we may neglect other important aspects of our lives: wifehood being one of them. I wanted to expand on this verse to emphasize that both motherhood and wifehood are sacred designations, and we are called to show up fully and wholeheartedly in each.

This verse highlights the importance and value of having a noble character, something more precious than rubies. To me, this means that our focus should be on cultivating a virtuous heart, rather than solely on physical appearance, job titles, accomplishments, or worldly achievements. A noble character must be rooted in Christ, and as we reflect this virtue, it positively impacts our relationships.

On the flip side, there are days when my confidence feels unshakable, and others when my body changes and the lack of time to dress up leaves me feeling less than my best. In those moments, being reminded that my worth is far greater than rubies is truly uplifting.

When we cultivate character in Christ, it strengthens our husbands' confidence in us, creating a peaceful and joyful home environment. That peace and contentment then naturally extends to how we parent our children, allowing us to nurture them for the glory of God.

Prayer

Heavenly Father,

Thank you for this word that reminds us to first pursue a noble character through you and our value is beyond rubies. We pray that, for those of us who are married, our husbands can see your reflection in us. And for those of us who aspire to be wives, may you cultivate and grow this gift in our hearts. May our character become a source of pure joy and satisfaction in our homes, so we can nurture the same virtue in our children.

In Jesus' name, Amen.

Reflections of Grace

✝ How do these words shape the way you see your value and identity as both a mother and a wife through God's eyes?

✝ What does it look like for you to live as a woman of noble character in the everyday moments and decisions you face?

✝ How does embracing the truth that your worth is "far more than rubies" influence how you view yourself, especially on the hard days when you feel weary or unseen?

_____

_____

_____

_____

_____

_____

_____

_____

_____

_____

_____

_____

_____

_____

CHAPTER
TWENTY-THREE

Wisdom at Home:
The Foundation of a Godly House

> 📖 **Proverbs 14:1**
>
> *"The wise woman builds her house, but with her own hands the foolish one tears hers down."*

W hat is wisdom?

Wisdom is the ability to know what to do and when to do it. It shapes the way we make decisions and take actions, guided by insight, discernment, and spiritual or moral principles.

So, what does it mean to be a wise woman?

A wise woman leans on patience and diligence to strengthen her home. She prioritizes nurturing relationships, cultivating peace, and managing resources with care, raising her children in love, and supporting her husband or family. These intentional choices bring stability, growth, and blessing into her household.

In contrast, a foolish woman, through careless words, poor decisions, neglect, or strife, can weaken and even destroy her home. The destruction may not always be physical such as separation or divorce, but it can be emotional, causing discouragement or division; spiritual, neglecting God's ways; or practical, wasting resources and creating instability.

I pray that we strive daily to be wise women and mothers, understanding that the strength of our households often depends on the choices we make.

Prayer

Heavenly Father,

We ask you to do new work in us and make us wise women in our homes. If in any way we have contributed to the weakening of our families, whether knowingly or unknowingly, we repent today. Grant us the wisdom, patience, and willingness to honor you in all that we say and do. Help us to be faithful stewards of our families, so our homes may flourish and reflect the goodness of the God we serve.

In Jesus' name, Amen.

Reflections of Grace

✝ How do you personally define wisdom in your role as a mother, and where do you most often seek it, through prayer, scripture, or Godly counsel?

✝ Are there habits, patterns, or choices in your daily life that might be unintentionally disrupting the peace and unity of your home?

✝ In what ways can you use your words and actions to bring life, encouragement, and harmony to your family, rather than criticism or negativity?

_____

_____

_____

_____

_____

_____

_____

_____

_____

_____

_____

_____

_____

_____

_____

_____

_____

_____

CHAPTER
TWENTY-FOUR
Passing the Torch of Godly Belief

📖 2 Timothy 1:5

"I am reminded of your sincere faith, which first lived in your grandmother Lois and your mother Eunice and now, I am sure, dwells in you as well."

These words were spoken by the Apostle Paul to Timothy, highlighting the faith that had lived in his family across generations. Paul encouraged Timothy in his own walk by affirming that the same faith also lived within him. To me, this is profound, it shows the lasting impact that being a Godly role model can have, on the lives of our children, leaving a legacy that continues to grow and flourish.

In this verse, what began with Timothy's grandmother was passed down to his mother, and then to Timothy himself, three generations of faithful living. Godly influence from mothers, family members, or mentors can shape a person's spiritual journey in ways that last far beyond a single lifetime. Imagine the joy as a mother when someone shares how your life has positively shaped your children's faith!

Now that I am a mother, this is my greatest aspiration: to inspire my children to serve the Lord wholeheartedly. Children today are profoundly shaped by the faith they see in their parents, grandparents, and others around them, through lived-out beliefs, prayer, love, and trust in God. This verse reminds us that faith is relational, modeled, and contagious. What we live out matters far more than what we merely say; our faith can inspire and shape those who come after us.

Prayer

Heavenly Father,

Thank you for reminding us that the Godly example we set for our children can shape not only their lives but the generations that follow. Give us endurance to seek your presence genuinely, to cultivate a personal relationship with you rather than focusing on performance. Help us, Lord, to lead our children by showing them what it means to live a life fully surrendered to you.

In Jesus' name, Amen.

Reflections of Grace

✟ How does this verse remind you of the lasting influence your faith can have on your children and beyond?

✟ As you reflect on your own life, what examples of faith from your mother, grandmother, or other role models continue to inspire you today?

✟ What kind of spiritual legacy do you hope to leave for your family, and what intentional steps can you begin taking now to build that foundation?

CHAPTER
TWENTY-FIVE

The Kingdom Belongs to the Childlike

> 📖 **Matthew 19:14**
>
> *"Let the little children come to me, and do not hinder them, for the kingdom of heaven belongs to such as these."*

When the disciples tried to push the children away, Jesus gently rebuked them. In doing so, He revealed His deep love and compassion for little ones. Imagine it, while crowds pressed in, eager to hear His teaching and witness His miracles, Jesus paused to welcome children. What a reminder to us that no one is too small or insignificant for His attention.

Life often pulls us in many directions, but the moments we miss with our children can never be regained. Jesus not only welcomed them; He also pointed to their qualities as examples for us. If we desire to enter the Kingdom of Heaven, we must be like children: trusting, dependent on God, and pure in heart.

This passage also urges us to guard our influence. Just like the disciples in this verse, we too can, at times, unintentionally place barriers between others and Christ, whether through judgment, neglect, hypocrisy, or discouragement. Instead, God calls us to be a source of grace and support: to nurture faith, encourage spiritual growth, and create space for both the little ones He has entrusted to us and for all who are seeking to draw closer to Him.

Prayer

Heavenly Father,

Open our eyes to see children as you see them: pure, innocent, and deeply treasured. Cultivate within us a childlike spirit marked by wonder, humility, and trust. May our words and actions guide both our children and those around us closer to you, and may we reflect the heart and compassion of Jesus in everything we do.

In Jesus' name, Amen.

Reflections of Grace

✞ How does this verse influence your understanding of your calling as a mother to guide your children toward Jesus?

✞ In what ways can you intentionally cultivate a home where your children feel safe, loved, and drawn to God's presence?

✝ How can you model a childlike faith in your own walk with the Lord, showing your children through your words and actions, what it truly means to trust Him wholeheartedly?

_____

_____

_____

_____

_____

_____

_____

_____

_____

_____

_____

_____

_____

_____

_____

_____

_____

_____

_____

CHAPTER
TWENTY-SIX

Touched and Blessed

> 📖 **Mark 10: 16**
>
> *"And he took the children in his arms, placed his hands on them and blessed them."*

The verse we reflect on this week follows Jesus' rebuke of the disciples who tried to turn children away, a moment we touched on in the previous chapter. It's striking that it was the parents who brought their children to Jesus, seeking His blessing. Can you imagine their disappointment when the disciples dismissed them?

But Jesus, full of compassion, corrected His disciples and welcomed the children into His arms. He didn't just allow them to come, He embraced them. He laid His hands on them and blessed them. This wasn't just a kind gesture; it was a powerful demonstration of God's heart for children: tender, personal, and full of love.

This scene reminds me of something I witnessed growing up, when baby dedications in the church were handled differently depending on whether the child was born into a married family or not. Children born to married parents were presented before the congregation, while others were quietly blessed in a back room. Even as a child, that never sat right with me. If you've ever experienced this personally, I want to say I'm truly sorry. It wasn't Jesus who rejected your child, it was us, flawed humans, who failed you.

But I thank God for the healing He is bringing to His Church. We are seeing more of His heart reflected in our communities today. Just as Jesus made no distinction, neither should we. All children are precious to Him. All are welcome.

And for us mothers, what a sweet assurance: God never rejects our children. Regardless of the circumstances surrounding their birth, they are fully loved, fully received, and fully blessed by Him.

Prayer

Heavenly Father,

Thank you for showing us that every child matters to you. Thank you for embracing them with open arms and blessing them without condition. Help us reflect that same love to the children around us so they grow up knowing they are deeply loved by you.

In Jesus' name, Amen.

Reflections of Grace

✝ How does it move your heart to picture Jesus gently holding and blessing the children?

✝ In what ways do you see His deep love for them reflected in your own calling as a mother?

✝ What practical steps can you take to create a home where your children feel safe to experience God's presence and love?

✝ How are you intentionally receiving Jesus' love and blessing in your own life so that it overflows into the way you nurture and care for your family?

CHAPTER
TWENTY-SEVEN

Every Child Matters to God

> 📖 **Matthew 18:10**
>
> *"See that you do not despise one of these little ones. For I tell you that their angels in heaven always see the face of my Father in heaven."*

Reading this verse was both eye-opening and deeply moving. As we reflect on God's immense love and compassion, especially for the most vulnerable among us, this passage offers a profound reminder: no one is too small or insignificant in God's Kingdom.

God issues a clear warning: not to despise, overlook, or mistreat children. Why? Because they are under His divine care. And not just in theory, this verse affirms that angels have been assigned to them, angels who stand in the presence of God with constant access to Him. These heavenly beings are ready to act on behalf of the little ones they guard.

What a powerful image: children surrounded by divine protection, watched over by angels who dwell in God's presence. As parents, caregivers, and believers, we often worry about the safety of those most precious to us. But this verse invites us to lay down our fears and rest in the guarantee that God's protection goes beyond anything we can humanly provide.

Let this be your confidence today: even when your children are out of your sight, they are never out of God's. They are guarded by heaven itself.

Prayer

Heavenly Father,

Thank you for your gracious love and the protection you give to our children. Thank you for assigning angels to watch over them, especially in a world where they are so vulnerable. Let this truth cast out our fear and anxiety, and may we trust fully in your care. We rest in the knowledge that our little ones are never alone.

In Jesus' name, Amen.

Reflections of Grace

✝ How does this verse influence the way you see your children and recognize their priceless worth in God's eyes?

✝ How does it comfort and encourage you to know that God loves them so deeply that their angels continually stand in His presence, watching over them?

_____

_____

_____

_____

_____

_____

_____

_____

_____

_____

_____

_____

_____

_____

_____

_____

_____

_____

_____

CHAPTER
TWENTY-EIGHT

Never Forgotten

📖 **Isaiah 49:15**

"Can a mother forget the baby at her breast and have no compassion for the child she has borne? Though she may forget, I will not forget you."

During the time I was able to breastfeed my son, I remember feeling the most incredible response: my milk would let down the moment I heard him cry. It was both amazing and shocking. It's one thing to study the letdown reflex and the role of oxytocin in such a reaction, but it's entirely another to experience it firsthand. As mothers, we share an extraordinary bond with our children, and our first instinct is always to protect, love, and nurture them.

But there's more. Sadly, not all mothers are able to exhibit these traits, sometimes due to past traumas, struggles with addiction, or other challenging circumstances. The Lord reminds us that even when children are emotionally or physically abandoned by their mothers, He will never forget them.

Another way to interpret this verse is for those of us who have estranged relationships with our own mothers and are navigating the pain and hurt that comes with it. The Lord does not forget you either. I cannot imagine the difficulty for mothers who, having experienced abandonment or rejection themselves, work tirelessly to break that cycle for their own children. Your efforts to give the love and care you lacked are nothing short of heroic. The Lord sees the courage and resilience it takes to give what you never received, and He wants to remind you that your children are never forgotten.

Prayer

Heavenly Father,

Thank you for instilling in us mothers the instinct to love, nurture, and protect our children. Thank you for reminding us that even if we experienced neglect or absence in our own childhoods, you never forgot us. Thank you for healing our hearts from the pain we endured and for giving us the strength to overcome past traumas so that we can be the loving mothers our children need.

In Jesus' name, Amen.

Reflections of Grace

✝ What does it mean to you to know that God's love is deeper, stronger, and more dependable than even a mother's natural love for her child?

✝ How does this truth bring you comfort and reassurance, reminding you of His unwavering presence and unfailing care in every season of your life?

_____

_____

_____

_____

_____

_____

_____

_____

_____

_____

_____

_____

_____

_____

_____

_____

_____

_____

_____

_____

CHAPTER
TWENTY-NINE
Strength for the Journey

📖 Isaiah 40:31

"But those who hope in the Lord will renew their strength. They will soar on wings like eagles; they will run and not grow weary, they will walk and not be faint."

It takes a mother to truly understand what being a mother really means. Motherhood is not just about showing up, it's about being fully present. We step into countless roles for our little ones: cook, chauffeur, teacher, nurse, problem-solver, handyman, you name it.

For my husband and I, parenting our son alone has been both enjoyable and exhausting. I know many others share this journey, yet each story is unique. This verse resonates deeply with me. Motherhood comes with seasons of fatigue, sleepless nights, and endless demands. Yet trusting in God equips us to persevere even when the road feels unending. He gives us the strength to rise above stress, worry, and discouragement, helping us see our circumstances with clarity and hope.

Some days, I feel like 24 hours just aren't enough. And I only have one child! Yet this verse reminds me that our strength as mothers does not depend solely on our own reserves. God renews our energy and endurance, empowering us to keep going.

Prayer

Heavenly Father,

What a blessing it is to know that our hope is in you alone, not in men. Thank you for this gentle reminder of hope, renewal, and strength. Thank you for giving us the power to rise above hassles and continue forward with energy, purpose, and love.

In Jesus' name, Amen.

Reflections of Grace

☦ How have you experienced God's renewal in past seasons of your life, and how can those memories encourage and strengthen you this week?

☦ What would it mean for you to "soar on wings like eagles" as a mother, rising above the challenges you face and viewing your circumstances through God's perspective?

_____

_____

_____

_____

CHAPTER

THIRTY

The Path of Selfless Love

📖 **Philippians 2: 3-4**

"Do nothing out of selfish ambition... consider others better than yourselves."

As mothers, caring for our children often feels instinctive. We naturally ensure those around us are well cared for, sometimes at the expense of our own needs. I cannot count the many times I made sure my son ate all his meals and drank enough water, while I hadn't yet done the same for myself.

This verse reminds mothers to approach our responsibilities with humility, putting the needs of our children and family above personal desires, not out of obligation, but from genuine love and care. When a mother values others above herself, she models empathy, kindness, and selflessness, teaching her children to treat others with respect and compassion.

Yet, when we pour so much of ourselves into others, it's easy to feel unappreciated or to compare ourselves with others. We must root our actions in love, not in the pursuit of human recognition. Philippians 2:3-4 reminds us that every act of selfless love is meaningful in God's eyes. Even small sacrifices reflect Christ-like humility and strengthen the spiritual foundation of our families.

While putting others first is vital, these verses do not call us to neglect ourselves. A mother's care is most effective when she also nurtures her own spiritual, emotional, and physical wellbeing.

Prayer

Heavenly Father,

Help us meet the demands of motherhood with genuine care and compassion, not for human validation or applause. Thank you for reminding us that while you call us to put others' needs above our own, we should not neglect ourselves. Help us find the balance to lead with humility, serve with love, and nurture our families in a way that reflects Christ's heart.

In Jesus' name, Amen.

Reflections of Grace

✝ In what areas of motherhood do you find it most challenging to place the needs of others before your own?

✝ How does this verse encourage you to approach your daily decisions with a heart of humility, especially as you balance your own needs with those of your children and family?

✞ When frustration or exhaustion sets in, what makes it difficult to serve your loved ones with grace and patience? How can you lean on God's strength and invite His grace into those moments, allowing Him to renew your heart and perspective?

_____

_____

_____

_____

_____

_____

_____

_____

_____

_____

_____

_____

_____

_____

_____

_____

_____

_____

_____

_____

CHAPTER
THIRTY-ONE

New Mercies Every Morning

📖 **Lamentations 3: 22-23**

"Because of the Lord's great love we are not consumed, for his compassions never fail. They are new every morning."

Have you ever felt inadequate or like a failure as a mother when you make a mistake, forget something, or don't complete a task on your to-do list for your children or family? I certainly have, more times than I could ever count. These verses remind us that each new day is a fresh opportunity to care for our children, even after days filled with mistakes, fatigue, or messes.

When you doubt your abilities, God's unwavering love assures you that no matter what struggles yesterday held, His compassion and guidance are available today. His mercies invite us to forgive our own missteps and trust that His strength is sufficient for each new day.

Just as God's faithfulness never fails, your role as a mother, though often challenging, holds lasting significance. The love and care you pour into your children become part of the rhythm of life that mirrors God's consistency.

Prayer

Heavenly Father,

Thank you for renewing your compassion toward us each morning. Thank you for reminding us that even when we falter in our duties as mothers, you encourage us to leave those failures behind and start fresh with you. Please continue to guide our steps as we learn from our mistakes and strive every day to be better mothers for our children than we were the day before.

In Jesus' name, Amen.

Reflections of Grace

✝ How does this verse inspire you to view each new day as a gift and a fresh opportunity to encounter God's love and mercy?

✝ What does it mean to you personally that His mercy is "new every morning"? In what ways can this truth bring calm and reassurance to your heart, especially during challenging seasons?

✝ Can you recall a recent moment when you felt God's compassion carrying you through? How did that experience deepen your faith and trust in Him?

_____

_____

_____

_____

_____

_____

_____

_____

_____

_____

_____

_____

_____

_____

_____

_____

_____

_____

_____

_____

CHAPTER
THIRTY-TWO

The Boldness to Ask, the Grace to Receive

> 📖 **James 1:5**
>
> *"If any of you lacks wisdom, let him ask of God, who gives generously to all without reproach, and it will be given to him."*

Every day, we mothers, face countless decisions, big and small, ranging from disciplining and nurturing to scheduling, teaching, and protecting our children. Each choice requires wisdom, yet this verse reminds us that true wisdom comes from God, not from our own strength or experience alone.

I remember when I first gave birth, the fear of making the wrong decisions for my son felt heavy. I worried that, as a first-time mom, I might do something that could hurt him. Even now, after gaining skills and confidence in caring for him, that sense of uncertainty hasn't fully disappeared, and I don't believe it ever will. Each new milestone brings fresh concerns and decisions.

Even when we feel inexperienced, tired, or unsure, God is ready to guide us. This verse encourages humility, it's okay to admit we don't have all the answers and to seek God's direction. His wisdom is generous and freely given; it doesn't depend on our perfection.

When deciding how to respond to a child's behavior, we can pray for discernment. When balancing work, home, and family responsibilities, we can ask God for clarity and guidance. When we feel emotionally exhausted, we can seek His wisdom in our words, actions, and patience.

The bottom line is this: in everything we face as mothers, we should turn to God first.

Prayer

Heavenly Father,

Thank you for always being available to guide us when we ask. We admit that we don't have everything figured out in this motherhood journey and constantly need your help. Thank you for generously giving us your wisdom to navigate every challenge, decision, and uncertainty as we raise our children.

In Jesus' name, Amen.

Reflections of Grace

✝ In what areas of motherhood do you feel most desperate for God's wisdom in this season?

✟ How does it bring you peace to know that He offers wisdom freely and without judgment whenever you ask?

✟ When you're faced with challenging parenting decisions, how can you intentionally pause, quiet your heart, and seek God's guidance before responding out of emotion or external pressure?

_____

_____

_____

_____

_____

_____

_____

_____

_____

_____

_____

_____

_____

_____

_____

_____

_____

_____

_____

CHAPTER
THIRTY-THREE

Rejoice, Pray, Repeat

 1 Thessalonians 5:16-17

"Rejoice always, pray continually, give thanks in all circumstances."

We are invited to cultivate hearts full of gratitude and joy, not because life is always easy, but because God's presence gives us every reason to rejoice. As mothers, we are called to intentionally notice the blessings woven into our daily lives: the laughter of our children, small victories, quiet moments of peace, even amidst the nuisances.

We are encouraged to pray continually, not only for ourselves and in solitude, but with and for our children: during car rides, while cooking, at bedtime, and in every ordinary moment. A heart anchored in gratitude shifts our perspective from frustration to faith, allowing us to see God's work in our children, our families, and in ourselves.

Joy, prayer, and gratitude are powerful tools to help us navigate the challenges of motherhood. By rejoicing, staying in constant prayer, and giving thanks, we anchor ourselves in God's presence, gain strength for our daily responsibilities, and model faith and thankfulness to our children.

Prayer

Heavenly Father,

We thank you for the joy that comes from you alone. Our hearts overflow with gratitude for all that you have done for us and our families. Thank you for sustaining us. We pray that you help us notice your hand in every part of this motherhood journey, big or small, and that we always find joy in spending time in your presence.

In Jesus' name, Amen.

Reflections of Grace

✝ What does it truly mean to you to "rejoice always" amid the ups and downs of motherhood?

✝ In which areas of your life do you find it most challenging to hold on to joy, and how can you invite God's presence into those moments?

✝ How might you begin to cultivate the habit of "praying continually" throughout your day, even in the middle of busy routines, unexpected interruptions, and overwhelming tasks?

✠ Finally, what blessings might you be overlooking right now that you can pause to recognize and thank God for this week?

_____

_____

_____

_____

_____

_____

_____

_____

_____

_____

_____

_____

_____

_____

_____

_____

_____

_____

_____

_____

_____

CHAPTER
THIRTY-FOUR

Covered and Kept

 Psalm 91:4

"He will cover you with his feathers, and under his wings you will find refuge; his faithfulness will be your shield and rampart."

What a lovely picture of protection, comfort, and unwavering care! Those qualities resonate deeply with the heart of motherhood. The image of being sheltered beneath God's feathers reminds mothers that we are never alone: He is watching over us and our children with tender care.

This verse offers profound reassurance: God is our refuge, a place of emotional, spiritual, and even physical rest. Like a rampart, a strong and unyielding wall of defense, His faithfulness stands guard over us, shielding us from fear, worry, and doubt.

This metaphor is more than comfort; it's a promise. God's protection extends not only to us but also to our children. Just as we care for them with fierce love, He cares for us with even greater tenderness and strength. It is an invitation to lean into His presence during both the joyful and challenging seasons of motherhood.

Prayer

Heavenly Father,

Thank you for being our refuge, our safe place to rest, renew our strength, and find peace. Thank you for faithfully providing for us and shielding our hearts from fear, insecurity, and discouragement as we navigate the journey of motherhood. We are grateful for your constant presence and the reassurance that we are never alone.

In Jesus' name, Amen.

Reflections of Grace

✞ In what areas of your life or motherhood do you most need to feel God's protection and covering right now?

✞ How have you witnessed His faithfulness guarding you and your family through past challenges and storms?

✞ What practical steps can you take to release worry and control, choosing instead to rest fully in God's care and trust His strength over your own?

_____

_____

_____

CHAPTER
THIRTY-FIVE

The Command to Courage

 Joshua 1:9

"Be strong and courageous. Do not be afraid; the Lord your God will be with you wherever you go."

Less than a year ago, my husband and I relocated to a new city. We knew it was God's timing and were blessed with a home, yet the move came with its share of fear. Moving as adults is one thing, but moving to a city where we knew no one, and with a toddler in tow, was another. It required significant adjustments.

This verse reminds us to face fear with confidence, knowing that God's presence can calm anxiety and renew hope. Motherhood is a 24/7 calling, and at times it can feel isolating. Yet God's guidance, protection, and strength are always with us, in the mundane routines, in stressful moments, and in joyful milestones alike. When life feels crushing, we can take comfort in knowing that God equips us for every moment.

Let courage replace fear in the decisions we make for our children. Trust that God is present not only in the big, life-changing decisions but also in the small, everyday acts of care and love.

Prayer

Heavenly Father,

Thank you for calling us to be strong and courageous, a strength that can only come through you. Thank you for reminding us not to be afraid, for you are with us wherever we go.

In Jesus' name, Amen.

Reflections of Grace

- ☩ In what areas of your life or motherhood do you most need the reminder to "be strong and courageous"?

- ☩ How does this verse bring you comfort and hope when you're facing challenges that feel overwhelming or beyond your strength to handle?

- ☩ What does it look like to live out courage and faith in a way that allows your children to witness God's strength working through you?

_____

_____

_____

CHAPTER
THIRTY-SIX

An Everlasting Love

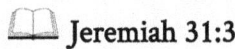 **Jeremiah 31:3**

"I have loved you with an everlasting love; I have drawn you with unfailing kindness."

As mothers, our children flourish in the love we show them daily. We are invited to love them as God loves us: faithfully, unconditionally, and without end. The words of this verse are God speaking to the children of Israel, reassuring them of His steadfast and unchanging love, even in the face of their rebellion. It is a love rooted not in merit, but in covenant, a divine love that is eternal, gracious, and unwavering.

Likewise, we are called to love our children not just through our actions, but also through our words.

Growing up, I never heard the words "I love you" from my parents. They showed love through provision and care, for which I was deeply grateful, but the absence of spoken affirmation left a void. Over time, I came to understand that they were simply passing down what they had received, or rather, what they hadn't. They, too, had never been told those words, and so didn't know how to give them.

What hurt most was the silence that followed discipline. Sometimes they would try to comfort me with my favorite snacks or kind gestures, and while I appreciated those efforts, the words still never came. Their love was real, but it was only ever shown, not spoken.

It's easy to fall into familiar patterns and unintentionally withhold from our children what we ourselves never received. But when we know better, we have a responsibility to do better. With intentionality and the strength God provides, we can break the cycle of generational curses and give our children the love we longed for growing up.

A mother's expression of love, both in word and deed, is essential. It creates emotional safety, builds trust, nurtures self-worth, and supports healthy development. Children need to know, without a doubt, that their mother's love is constant, even in difficult moments.

Love is not passive. It shows up, in presence, in patience, and in persistence. And even when it's hard, that steady, faithful love is what shapes secure, confident, and emotionally resilient children.

Prayer

Heavenly Father,

Thank you for reminding us that the love our children need is not a perfect love, but a faithful one. Help us to continue showing up for them with a love that is unconditional, steady, forgiving, and present.

May we mirror the everlasting love you have shown us, leaving a lasting imprint on our children's hearts and souls.

In Jesus' name, Amen.

Reflections of Grace

✝ When you reflect on God's everlasting love, what emotions or memories rise to the surface?

✝ How have you personally experienced His gentle kindness drawing you closer to Him?

✝ In what areas of your life, or motherhood, do you need to be reminded today that God's love remains constant, unchanging, and unconditional?

_____

_____

_____

_____

_____

_____

_____

_____

_____

_____

CHAPTER
THIRTY-SEVEN

Tired Hands, Hopeful Heart

 Galatians 6:9

"Let us not grow weary in doing good, for at the proper time we will reap a harvest if we do not give up."

I still remember the moment I found out I was pregnant with my son. In what felt like the blink of an eye, nine months passed, and the long-anticipated day of his birth arrived. I also vividly recall those early postpartum days: the sleepless nights, the constant cycle of breastfeeding, pumping, diaper changes, and everything in between.

Now, that tiny baby is a toddler, full of energy and curiosity, running around and growing before my eyes.

Recently, this verse struck a deep chord in my heart: Galatians 6:9: "Let us not grow weary in doing good, for at the proper time we will reap a harvest if we do not give up."

As mothers, we often find ourselves doing the same tasks day in and day out: laundry, dishes, meals, school drop-offs, help with homework, etc. This verse reminds us that these consistent, loving efforts are not in vain.

Motherhood is a long-term investment. We're planting seeds of love, character, and stability: seeds that may not sprout right away, but in time, will bear beautiful fruit in our children's lives. Whether we're teaching them values, guiding them through challenges, or simply showing up every day, we're sowing into their future.

Galatians 6:9 offers encouragement and hope. It reminds us to stay faithful, to persevere, and to trust that God is working, often behind the scenes, in the hearts of our children.

Prayer

Heavenly Father,

When I feel weary or wonder if I'm making a difference, help me remember that my efforts matter. Your word in Galatians 6:9 assures me that the seeds I sow today will one day produce a harvest. Give me strength to keep going, even when the results aren't immediate. Help me to trust that you are honoring the work I'm doing in my children's lives.

In Jesus' name, Amen.

Reflections of Grace

✝ What does it look like for you to "do good" in this season of life, as a mother, wife, or friend?

✟ How have you witnessed small, faithful actions in your home or relationships grow and bear fruit over time, even when the results didn't come right away?

✟ When you feel weary or tempted to give up, which promises from God can you cling to for strength and encouragement?

✟ How does trusting in His perfect timing fill you with hope as you wait for the beautiful "harvest" He has prepared?

_____

_____

_____

_____

_____

_____

_____

_____

_____

_____

_____

_____

_____

_____

_____

_____

CHAPTER
THIRTY-EIGHT

Give Thanks Anyway

 1 Thessalonians 5:18

"Give thanks in all circumstances; for this is God's will for you in Christ Jesus."

Parenting is filled with moments that warm your heart, like the days when my son is happy, playful, and we share sweet memories together. I've learned to soak in those precious times and hold them close.

But there are also days when it feels like a storm won't pass, when my son is teething and in pain, when he's constipated and uncomfortable, when the house is a mess, emotions are running high, and I'm consoling him from one meltdown to the next. In those harder moments, I've been learning to do something different: to praise and worship God right in the middle of the chaos.

Worship has always been something I enjoy, I could sing all day long. But choosing to worship in the midst of stress or fatigue? When I do it, I find myself calmer, more grounded. It shifts my perspective and helps me respond with grace rather than frustration. It doesn't mean I always get it right. In fact, I often don't.

Just recently, after working an overnight shift, I was desperate for rest. My son refused to nap, no matter what I tried, and I had another shift coming up that evening. Exhausted, I brought him to my husband's office, handed him off, and shut the door, telling my husband I had to sleep. Later that night at work, I felt a wave of guilt, wondering if I could've handled things differently.

But even in moments like that, I'm reminded of the power of gratitude. There's a verse that encourages us not necessarily to be thankful for every situation, but to be thankful in every situation. That's a profound difference. When the baby won't stop crying and the house is a wreck, I can still give thanks that I have a child to love and a home to care for.

Finding joy and gratitude in the everyday moments of motherhood, especially the hard and ordinary ones, isn't always easy. When gratitude feels impossible, He reminds us we're not alone. He is our peace, our patience, and our perspective.

Prayer

Heavenly Father,

Thank you for calling us to practice gratitude not just as a feeling, but as a spiritual discipline. Thank you for anchoring our hearts in hope, strengthening our spirits, and drawing us closer to you, even in the messiest moments of motherhood.

In Jesus' name, Amen.

Reflections of Grace

✞ What are three blessings, whether big or small, that you can pause to thank God for this week?

✞ How does embracing gratitude as part of God's will bring clarity and peace to your heart?

✞ This week, who can you intentionally thank or encourage as a way to reflect God's love and kindness?

_____

_____

_____

_____

_____

_____

_____

_____

_____

_____

_____

_____

_____

_____

_____

CHAPTER
THIRTY-NINE

The Right Hand of Assurance

>  Isaiah 41:13
>
> *"For I am the Lord your God who takes hold of your right hand and says to you, do not fear; I will help you."*

As mothers, we often feel the weight of being strong for everyone around us. It can seem as though we are not allowed to have a bad day, or to step back from the many roles we juggle. We are natural multitaskers, constantly carrying more than meets the eye. Just because we carry it well doesn't mean it's not heavy. That is the truth of motherhood, we, too, experience fear, insecurity, and doubt, just like anyone else.

I've had countless moments when I've felt those emotions, and even more beyond them. Returning to the workforce after having my son for example, was one of the hardest transitions I've ever faced. I remember crying the first time I left for work, feeling a tight knot in my heart as I walked out the door. In that moment, I had to remind myself that going to work was part of my calling as his parent, to help provide and create a secure future for him. Deep down, I carried a quiet fear that I might miss some of his precious milestones: his first words, his first steps, and those once-in-a-lifetime memories that can never be repeated.

Now that he's a toddler, there are days when he cries as he watches me leave. Those moments tug deeply at my heart, but I push forward, knowing he is safe and deeply loved in my husband's care. When I come home, I do my best to be fully present with him, cherishing every laugh, hug, and story shared, as if I'm trying to make up for the hours spent apart while I'm away at work.

God treats us with the same tenderness, care, patience, and compassion we pour into our little ones. On sleepless nights, remember: God is holding your hand. In moments of guilt or failure, know that He is your helper, not your accuser. He is always near, holding your hand with gentleness and love.

Prayer

Heavenly Father,

What a blessed promise it is to know that you hold our hand every step of the way. Thank you for reminding us through your word that because you are guiding us, we have no reason to fear, as we walk in the same role of guiding and caring for our children.

In Jesus' name, Amen.

Reflections of Grace

✟ How does it bring you comfort to imagine God gently holding your hand and walking beside you through life's most difficult seasons?

✟ In what ways can you remind both your children and yourself that He is always near, ready to help, guide, and strengthen you?

✟ When fear begins to rise, which scripture or truth can you hold tightly to, keeping your heart steady and anchored in God's unchanging promises?

_____

_____

_____

_____

_____

_____

_____

_____

_____

_____

_____

CHAPTER

FORTY

The Garments of the Heart

> 📖 **Colossians 3:12–14**
>
> *"Therefore, as God's chosen people, holy and dearly loved, clothe yourselves with compassion, kindness, humility, gentleness and patience... And over all these virtues put on love, which binds them all together in perfect unity."*

D id you know that before you are a mom, wife, or caregiver, you are first and foremost God's chosen, holy, and dearly loved child? This verse reminds us of our true identity.

Each day, as we get up and prepare for the day ahead, we carefully choose what clothes to wear. In the same way, we must also clothe ourselves spiritually. What does that mean? It means intentionally choosing to respond with compassion, kindness, humility, gentleness, and patience, even in the midst of the beautiful chaos of motherhood.

Our children are learning and growing just as we are. They, too, need grace and understanding. Family life can be messy, filled with misunderstandings, whether with your children, your spouse, or even within your own heart. This verse calls us to practice forgiveness freely, just as Christ has forgiven us. When we extend that kind of grace, we model for our children what true love and mercy look like in action.

At the heart of it all is love. Love is more than a fleeting emotion; it's a deliberate choice and a powerful force that binds our families together. It sustains unity, nurtures peace, and strengthens the bond we share with our children.

Take this as your reminder: God has already clothed you with His Spirit, equipping you to reflect His heart in your home. He has provided everything you need.

Prayer

Heavenly Father,

Thank you for calling me your beloved. Help me to begin each day by clothing myself with compassion, kindness, humility, gentleness, and patience. When I am weary, remind me of your strength. When frustration rises, cover me with your peace. Above all, let your love guide my actions and words so that my home reflects your heart.

In Jesus' name, Amen.

Reflections of Grace

✝ Which of these qualities: compassion, kindness, humility, gentleness, and patience comes most naturally for you to live out, and which one do you find most challenging?

✝ How might it shift your perspective to remember that you are God's chosen, holy, and dearly loved before you interact with your family each day?

✝ Are there any lingering conflicts or hurts within your home that need to be addressed with forgiveness?

✝ How does reflecting on God's abundant forgiveness toward you inspire you to extend grace to your spouse, children, or others in your life?

_____

_____

_____

_____

_____

_____

_____

_____

_____

_____

CHAPTER
FORTY-ONE

The Gentle Shepherd's Care

📖 **Isaiah 40:11**

"He tends his flock like a shepherd: He gathers the lambs in his arms and carries them close to his heart; he gently leads those that have young."

To truly grasp the depth of this verse, we must first understand what it means to be a shepherd. A shepherd is far more than someone who simply tends sheep. He carefully guides them to safe pastures, ensures they have food and water, protects them from harm, and watches over their overall well-being.

Does that sound familiar? It should, this image takes us back to Psalm 23, which wonderfully portrays the heart of a shepherd. In Isaiah's time, these words were written to bring hope to the people of Israel during a season of hardship and exile, reminding them of God's unfailing compassion and power.

As mothers, these words speak deeply to us as well. God sees the unique burdens we carry as caregivers. Like a loving shepherd, He guards, guides, and nurtures us. His care is tender, His love unending, and His guidance steady.

Prayer

Heavenly Father,

Thank you for being our Good Shepherd. You lead us with gentleness and compassion, giving us the strength and wisdom we need each day. Thank you for holding us close to your heart and for faithfully providing for us as we care for our children.

In Jesus' name, Amen.

Reflections of Grace

✝ How have you experienced God's gentle hand guiding you throughout your journey of motherhood?

✝ In what ways can you find peace and rest in knowing that He is your faithful shepherd, lovingly caring for both you and your children?

✝ What does it mean to your heart to know that God leads you with tenderness, never rushing or harshly pushing, while you nurture and care for the precious lives He has entrusted to you?

CHAPTER
FORTY-TWO

Love that Overcomes All

> 📖 **Romans 8:38-39**
>
> *"For I am convinced that neither death nor life, neither angels nor demons, neither the present nor the future, nor any powers, neither height nor depth, nor anything else in all creation, will be able to separate us from the love of God that is in Christ Jesus our Lord."*

This is a verse that many Christians know well, but it speaks powerfully to mothers too. It reminds us that nothing, not even our worst day, can separate us from God's love. His love covers us when we lose our patience, when guilt whispers that we aren't doing enough, and when we're stretched thin by endless responsibilities.

As mothers, we all face moments of discouragement and "mom-guilt." I know this struggle personally as a working mom, where the weight of guilt can feel extremely burdensome. Yet this passage is a reminder that God's love is constant and complete. Whether you're caring for a newborn, navigating toddler tantrums, parenting a teenager, or watching your grown children step into the world, His love remains unchanging.

There will be seasons when motherhood feels lonely, when financial burdens weigh on you, or when relationships are strained. In those times, cling to this truth: God's love is deeper than your deepest pain and higher than your greatest joy.

Prayer

Heavenly Father,

Thank you for the powerful reminder that your love is unshakable and secured in your unchanging character. You love us when we are hard on ourselves and when we feel like we're failing. Thank you for carrying our guilt, our fears, and our negative thoughts. Help us to rest in the affirmation that nothing can ever separate us from your perfect love.

In Jesus' name, Amen.

Reflections of Grace

✝ How does it impact you personally to know that nothing, not even your mistakes, fears, or failures can separate you from God's love?

✝ Are there lies you've believed about your identity or worth that this truth helps to silence and replace with God's promises?

✝ As you reflect on this passage, how does it move your heart to worship and express gratitude for His unwavering faithfulness and grace?

_____

_____

_____

_____

_____

_____

_____

_____

_____

_____

_____

_____

_____

_____

_____

_____

_____

_____

_____

CHAPTER
FORTY-THREE

A Mother's Moral Compass

 **Proverbs 11:3**

"The integrity of the upright guides them, but the unfaithful are destroyed by their duplicity."

Integrity is about living with honesty and consistency, making choices that are firmly rooted in truth and guided by Godly values. When we walk in integrity, our decisions are shaped by God's wisdom.

Our integrity doesn't just influence our personal choices; it sets the tone for our entire household. Children look to their mothers for direction, stability, and a sense of security. When we model a life built on God's principles, we create an environment where they can flourish, develop strong character, and grow in their own faith.

This becomes especially important when facing difficult decisions, whether it's how to discipline, manage finances, or spend precious time as a family. Integrity ensures that our choices reflect our faith and values, even when it's hard or inconvenient.

Proverbs 11:3 also warns us about duplicity, saying one thing while doing another, or living in a way that contradicts what we claim to believe. Such inconsistency can confuse our children, erode their trust, and ultimately damage relationships within our home. A lack of integrity opens the door to frustration, hurt, and division, while a life of integrity fosters harmony, trust, and respect.

Prayer

Heavenly Father,

Help me to walk faithfully and with integrity. May every decision I make as a mother reflect your truth and grace. Guard my heart against duplicity so that my words and actions align with your will. Let my life be a living example of honesty, faithfulness, and love, creating a home filled with peace, trust, and your presence.

In Jesus' name, Amen.

Reflections of Grace

✝ How does this verse inspire you to trust that God will honor your faithfulness as you walk in His ways?

✝ Can you recall a time when choosing integrity, though challenging in the moment, resulted in experiencing God's blessing, guidance, or protection?

_____

_____

CHAPTER
FORTY-FOUR

For Such a Time as This

📖 Esther 4:14

"And who knows but that you have come to your royal position for such a time as this?"

This verse holds a deeply personal and powerful reminder: your role as a mother is no accident, it is part of God's intentional and perfect plan. Just as Esther was placed in her royal position to save her people, you have been placed in your family, in this very season of life, for a divine purpose.

God chose you to be the mother of your specific children, fully knowing the world they would grow up in and the challenges they would face. He entrusted you to guide, nurture, and love them through it all. Never forget that your prayers, sacrifices, and daily acts of care are woven into a greater story, one that is shaping generations according to His will. None of it is meaningless.

Like Esther, you may not fully see the weight of your influence right now, but your faithfulness leaves a lasting impact. When the demands of motherhood feel intense, let this verse be a gentle whisper to your heart: "You were chosen for this family, these children, and this very moment."

Prayer

Heavenly Father,

Thank you for choosing me to be a mother to these precious children. When the weight of responsibility feels heavy, remind me that you have called and equipped me for this role. Help me to trust your plan, even when I cannot see the full picture. Strengthen my heart, renew my spirit, and let my faithfulness leave a lasting legacy for my children.

In Jesus' name, Amen.

Reflections of Grace

✝ When feelings of inadequacy or doubt creep in, how can you hold onto the truth that God equips and strengthens those He calls?

✝ In what areas of your life might He be inviting you to step out with courage and faith, trusting that He has placed you "for such a time as this"?

✝ Who is God prompting you to encourage, protect, or boldly stand up for, following Esther's example of bravery and obedience?

CHAPTER
FORTY-FIVE

A Present Help

> 📖 **Psalm 46:1**
>
> *"God is our refuge and strength, a very present help in trouble."*

God lovingly offers Himself as a safe refuge, a place to run when the emotional weight of motherhood feels overwhelming, when exhaustion sets in, and when you simply need a break. Just as a physical shelter provides protection from a storm, God provides emotional and spiritual covering when the challenges of raising children feel too much to bear.

When life feels chaotic and out of control, pause and remember: you are never alone. God is your hiding place, the source of rest and renewed peace. In those moments when you feel completely drained, whisper a simple prayer: "Lord, be my strength today." With those words, you shift the weight from your own shoulders to His capable hands.

The time when we were transitioning from one city to another was incredibly stressful. We were on a tight deadline to vacate our condo, I was preparing to start a new job, and we needed to settle into our new home, all at once. My husband and I didn't know how we were going to manage everything, but we chose to put our trust in God, our refuge and strength.

God not only gave us peace and strength spiritually, but He also sent tangible help through family and friends. They stepped in to support us, helping with the move, caring for our son, and making the transition into our new home so much smoother. We are forever grateful for their love, kindness, and willingness to walk alongside us during that season. When we place our trust in God as our strength, He reveals Himself in ways far beyond anything we could ever imagine or expect.

This verse reminds us of the truth that we can run to God daily, drawing on His strength and trusting in His constant presence. He is with us in every moment of motherhood, offering peace when we feel scattered and strength when we feel weak.

Prayer

Heavenly Father,

Thank you for being my refuge and my ever-present help throughout this journey of motherhood. Thank you for the comforting reminder that I can come to you anytime the load feels difficult to bear and trust you to renew my strength. In the chaos of motherhood, teach me to lean fully on you, finding rest, hope, and endurance in your presence.

In Jesus' name, Amen.

Reflections of Grace

✝ Where do you naturally turn for comfort and safety when stress, anxiety, or overwhelm start to rise? How can you make a conscious choice to turn to God first, instead of relying on temporary fixes?

✝ When life feels chaotic or uncertain, what does it mean to you personally to know that God is your true refuge?

✝ Can you remember a time when you felt completely weak and powerless, yet experienced God carrying you through with His strength and faithfulness?

_____

_____

_____

_____

_____

_____

_____

_____

CHAPTER
FORTY-SIX

The Bigger Picture

📖 **Romans 8:28**

"And we know that for those who love God all things work together for good, for those who are called according to his purpose."

This is a powerful perspective that speaks directly into the highs and lows of motherhood. We've come to understand that motherhood is more than just a role, it's a divine calling. The verse highlights those who are "called according to His purpose," reminding us that every act of love, every moment of discipline, every nurturing word, and even every tear is part of God's greater plan.

There's no better place to plant seeds of love, tenderness, compassion, forgiveness, patience, and the fruits of the Spirit than in the hearts of our children. Every moment you pour into their growth and development matters. Take heart knowing that you are sowing into the most meaningful ground, and what you plant today will bear fruits for years to come.

Motherhood is sacred work. Whatever challenges you may face along the way, God is able to redeem them, to bring growth, healing, and transformation through them. The verse says, "we know," not "we hope," that's a promise, not a possibility. The "good" it speaks of may not always look the way we expect, but it is always shaped by His perfect love and purpose.

Prayer

Heavenly Father,

Thank you for being present in every part of my journey as a mother. Even when I can't see the outcome, help me to trust that you are working through every moment, every joy, and every hardship for something greater. Thank you for the assurance that all things are truly working together for my good.

In Jesus' name, Amen.

Reflections of Grace

✝ How does the truth that God's plan is greater than your current circumstances bring peace and reassurance to your heart?

✝ Can you think of a time when God took a challenging situation from your past and used it to bring growth, healing, or unexpected blessings?

✝ Who in your life might need to be encouraged by this same hope this week, and how can you share it with them in a meaningful way?

_____

_____

_____

_____

_____

_____

_____

_____

_____

_____

_____

_____

_____

_____

_____

_____

_____

_____

_____

CHAPTER
FORTY-SEVEN
Pressure that Produces Purpose

📖 **James 1:2-3**

"Consider it pure joy, my brothers and sisters, whenever you face trials of many kinds, because you know that the testing of your faith produces perseverance."

Instead of viewing trials as setbacks, we can see them as opportunities for growth and transformation. These words don't call us to put on a mask of false happiness when life feels draining. Rather, they invite us to experience a deeper, lasting joy, one that is firmly rooted in God's purpose and the fruit that comes through perseverance.

For mothers, this means recognizing that every sleepless night, every difficult decision, and every act of sacrifice is shaping us. Our patience is being stretched, our love is deepening, and our character is being refined day by day. These are not just hard moments; they are sacred spaces where our faith comes alive.

Don't we all wish our children would behave perfectly everywhere and at all times? While that may sound wonderful, it's simply not realistic, and placing those expectations on ourselves or our children only lead to unnecessary pressure and stress.

Our son, like most toddlers, absolutely loves being outside. But as toddlers do, after a while, he wants to wander, explore, play, or sometimes gets cranky when he's tired, hungry, or needs to be changed.

To others, these moments might look like misbehavior, when in reality, he's just being a toddler. Still, I sometimes catch myself worrying about how his behavior might be interpreted. Those situations can bring feelings of embarrassment and uncertainty about how to handle them in the moment, which can easily test my patience.

As we endure the pressures and unpredictable rhythms of motherhood, our trust in God grows stronger. When we choose to love, to serve, and to lean on Him amid the chaos, we are building a perseverance that leads to maturity in our faith.

Prayer

Heavenly Father,

Thank you for the moments of motherhood that challenge and shape me. Help me to see them not as burdens, but as opportunities for spiritual growth. Thank you that even in the messiness, you are producing strength, perseverance, and a deeper dependence on you.

Continue your good work in me as I navigate this beautiful, demanding journey of motherhood. In Jesus' name, Amen.

Reflections of Grace

✞ Can you recall a time when walking through a difficult season deepened your faith and drew you closer to God?

✞ How does remembering that He can bring beauty and purpose out of every trial help you remain hopeful and steady in the midst of challenges?

✞ In what ways can you show your children that true joy is found in God's presence, rather than in having everything go perfectly?

_____

_____

_____

_____

_____

_____

_____

_____

_____

_____

_____

CHAPTER
FORTY-EIGHT

No Greater Joy

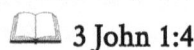 3 John 1:4

"I have no greater joy than to hear that my children are walking in the truth."

There is a profound spiritual and practical meaning in this verse. As mothers, we long to see our children thrive, not just physically or academically, but spiritually. It reflects the deepest joy of parenting: knowing that our children are growing in their relationship with God and living according to His truth.

While achievements like good grades, sports trophies, or other milestones are wonderful, they are temporary. This verse calls us to focus on what truly lasts, raising children who love, know, and walk with the Lord. When our children begin to live out the truths we've planted in their hearts, it becomes a beautiful return on our labor of love and sacrifice.

I encourage you to pray daily for your children's spiritual growth, even when the results aren't immediately visible. Model a life of faith by living out the very truths you teach, and celebrate the small victories along the way, like a kind word, an act of honesty, or the simple moment when your child chooses to pray on their own.

As young as my son is, he knows to clap his hands or shout "yay!" whenever he accomplishes something good. In the same way, my prayer is that his heart will overflow with that same joy as he grows in his personal walk with Christ, finding true delight in following Him.

Prayer

Heavenly Father,

Thank you for the precious gift of motherhood. Grant me wisdom and patience as I guide my children, so they may walk faithfully in your truth. Remind me that every act of love and faithfulness, no matter how small, has eternal value. May my greatest joy be found in watching my children grow closer to you each day.

In Jesus' name, Amen.

Reflections of Grace

✟ How can you intentionally pause to celebrate the small, everyday ways you see God at work in your children's hearts and lives?

✟ In what ways does this verse capture your deepest hopes and prayers for your children, or for those you nurture and influence?

✝ As you reflect on their spiritual growth, what fills your heart with the greatest sense of joy and gratitude?

_____

_____

_____

_____

_____

_____

_____

_____

_____

_____

_____

_____

_____

_____

_____

_____

_____

_____

_____

_____

_____

_____

_____

CHAPTER
FORTY-NINE

Renewed Thinking,
Renewed Motherhood

> 📖 **2 Corinthians 10:5**
>
> *"We demolish arguments and every pretension that sets itself up against the knowledge of God, and we take captive every thought to make it obedient to Christ."*

Did you know that through Christ, you have the authority to take control of your thoughts instead of allowing them to control you? Our thoughts are powerful. They can weigh heavily on our hearts and deeply influence how we parent and respond to our children. That's why it's so important to be intentional about capturing negative thoughts and replacing them with God's truth.

Instead of letting your mind spiral into worry, fear, or self-criticism, pause and refocus on what God says about you and your role as a mother. For example, a defeating thought might be: "I'm not patient enough to handle my toddler." Replace it with this truth: "God's grace is sufficient for me, and His strength is made perfect in my weakness" (2 Corinthians 12:9).

When you practice taking your thoughts captive, you're not just guarding your own heart, you're modeling a powerful habit for your children. When they see you pray out loud over your worries or speak scripture in challenging moments, they learn that God's Word is a weapon against fear and negativity. This gives them a strong foundation for their own faith as they grow.

When a negative thought enters your mind, don't let it take root. Pause, take a deep breath, and pray: "Lord, I surrender this thought to you. Replace it with your truth."

Identify the lies the enemy whispers and combat them with God's Word. Write down verses that speak directly to your situation and repeat them throughout the day until His truth becomes your focus.

Fill your home with words that uplift and inspire. Encourage your children by speaking promises from scripture, even when circumstances feel challenging. Let your words plant seeds of faith, hope, and love in their hearts.

Prayer

Heavenly Father,

Help me to take captive every thought that does not align with your word. When fear, doubt, or guilt try to take root, remind me that your truth is my weapon. Teach me to speak life over myself, my children, and my family. Let my mind be a place of peace, faith, and victory through you.

In Jesus' name, Amen.

Reflections of Grace

☩ Which thoughts tend to weigh you down the most: fear, doubt, guilt, comparison, or something else?

☩ How does this verse inspire you to be more intentional about which thoughts you allow to take root in your heart and mind?

☩ What does it look like for you personally to "take every thought captive" and surrender it to Christ?

☩ How does knowing that, through His strength, you can overcome destructive thought patterns bring you hope and encouragement this week?

_____

_____

_____

_____

_____

_____

_____

_____

CHAPTER
FIFTY

Victory through Christ

 1 Corinthians 15:57

"But thanks be to God! He gives us victory through our Lord Jesus Christ."

No matter the challenges, weariness, or battles we face in everyday life, victory has already been secured through Jesus Christ. We must try to shift our focus from our struggles to God's unshakable power and abundant grace.

As mothers, we often carry feelings of inadequacy or frustration, moments when our patience wears thin or when we feel like we're falling short of meeting every need. But we don't have to fight those thoughts alone, because Jesus has already overcome them. His victory doesn't mean that life will always be easy, but it does mean we don't have to fight in our own strength.

As I sit here writing, the timeless hymn "Victory in Jesus" fills my heart and mind. Its words beautifully capture the essence of the gospel: a loving Savior who sought us, redeemed us with His precious blood, and walks faithfully beside us through every season of life.

This week, let this song be more than just a familiar melody. May it serve as a powerful reminder that no matter the challenges we face, our victory has already been secured through Jesus. In Him, we can stand confident and unshaken, knowing that His triumph is our triumph, today and always.

Through the Holy Spirit, we are empowered to be the mothers our children need, even on the hardest days. At times, motherhood can feel like living in constant battle mode, but this verse reminds us that the battle is already won. We don't have to strive for perfection; instead, we are called to lean on Christ, who brings true and lasting victory.

Prayer

Heavenly Father,

Thank you for giving me victory through Jesus. Help me to release my fears, guilt, and doubts, and to rest in your grace. Strengthen me each day, and remind me that I am never fighting alone. Teach me to believe that, through you, I am enough and that I am doing what is right for my children.

In Jesus' name, Amen.

Reflections of Grace

✝ How does knowing that Jesus has already won the victory for you change the way you approach your daily struggles and spiritual battles?

✝ What does it look like to live with confidence and peace, knowing that through Christ, you are already victorious?

✝ How can sharing your personal story of God's faithfulness bring hope to someone who feels defeated or discouraged?

✝ What simple act of love, service, or encouragement can you offer this week to reflect Christ's victory and point others to His power and grace?

_____

_____

_____

_____

_____

_____

_____

_____

_____

_____

_____

_____

_____

_____

_____

_____

_____

_____

_____

_____

_____

_____

_____

_____

_____

_____

_____

_____

_____

_____

_____

_____

_____

CHAPTER
FIFTY-ONE
Encouraged in the Lord

📖 1 Samuel 30:6

"But David encouraged himself in the Lord his God."

In this passage, David found himself in a deeply distressing situation, his people had turned against him, and he had suffered great loss. Yet, instead of collapsing under the weight of it all, he chose to encourage himself in the Lord. This moment stands as a timeless example, especially for us mothers, who often feel stretched beyond our limits.

Motherhood is a sacred assignment, and God has given us grace to walk it out. We often ask others for grace too: whether it's a helping hand, patience when we take too long to return a message, or understanding when we seem distant. But just as important, we must remember to extend grace to ourselves.

Has this ever happened to you? You're having one of those rough days, barely holding it together, when suddenly your child does something so simple yet so powerful: like flashing a sweet smile, wrapping their tiny arms around you, gazing at you with a look that seems to reach deep into your soul, or saying something so funny it makes you burst into laughter. At that moment, everything shifts. Suddenly, the chaos fades, and you feel like the most important person in the world. Every time this happens, I'm reminded that, in my child's eyes, I am the perfect mom.

We've talked about how motherhood demands constant strength, even on the days when we're exhausted, overlooked, or simply worn down. Like David, we can turn inward and upward, encouraging ourselves in God.

I invite you to take a moment each day to pause, breathe, and speak life over yourself. Encourage yourself in the Lord. Give yourself grace. You're doing your best, and even when it doesn't feel like enough, remember this: you are a great mom.

Prayer

Heavenly Father,

Thank you for the example of David, who encouraged himself in you when everything around him seemed to fall apart. Help us to do the same in our journey of motherhood. Teach us to show ourselves the same grace we so freely offer to and ask from others. Remind us that we are doing our best each day, for our children, and our families. Strengthen us for the roles we carry: as mothers, wives, daughters, sisters, aunties, employees, and most importantly, as your daughters.

In Jesus' name, Amen.

Reflections of Grace

✝ In what areas of your life do you carry the weight of others' expectations or disappointments?

✝ When you feel misunderstood, criticized, or alone, what scripture or truth can you hold tightly to for strength and reassurance?

_____

_____

_____

_____

_____

_____

_____

_____

_____

_____

_____

_____

_____

_____

_____

_____

CHAPTER
FIFTY-TWO

The Promise of Restoration

> 📖 **1 Peter 5:10**
>
> *"And the God of all grace, who called you to his eternal glory in Christ, after you have suffered a little while, will himself restore you and make you strong, firm and steadfast."*

Ask yourself this: What is your ultimate goal as a mother? After raising your children through physical exhaustion, emotional highs and lows, sleepless nights, endless giving, worries about their health and future, and balancing work and home, what do you truly desire when all is said and done? These are profound questions we must honestly ask ourselves.

As we continue to nurture our children with patience, guide our families through inconveniences, and remain steadfast in faith, even when doubts or fears arise, this verse invites us into a deeper relationship with God, a relationship that leads to eternal life and sharing in His glory. The hardships of raising our children are temporary, and our hearts' prayers and desires should focus on the hope that one day we, along with our families, will experience God's presence forever.

What a glorious day it will be to stand before our Almighty God, hand in hand with our families and our children, and hear Him say: "Well done, good and faithful servant. You have been faithful with a few things; come and share in your Master's joy!" (Matthew 25:21).

Prayer

Heavenly Father,

Thank you for restoring, strengthening, and equipping us to love and guide our children. We ask for your mercy, Lord, and that the labor of our hearts and hands may not be in vain. Teach us how to raise our children according to your ways, and when you call us home, may we and our families, our children included, be welcomed into your loving arms forever. This is the desire of our hearts. We ask it not because we are worthy, but in the name of your son, Jesus Christ.

In Jesus' name, Amen.

Reflections of Grace

✝ Are there areas of your life, heart, or family where you deeply long to see God bring healing and restoration?

✟ What does it mean to you personally to know that God is truly "the God of all grace," meeting you with love and mercy in every season?

✟ When you walk through trials, how does it encourage your heart to remember that your suffering is only temporary, especially in light of the eternal glory and joy that God has promised?

_____

_____

_____

_____

_____

_____

_____

_____

_____

_____

_____

_____

_____

_____

_____

_____

Final Words
of Encouragement

As you turn the final page of this devotional, carry this truth with you: you are deeply loved, fully known, and never alone. Motherhood is a journey filled with breathtaking highs and challenging lows, yet through it all, God's grace remains constant and unshakable.

There will be days when you feel strong, joyful, and capable, and others when you feel weary and uncertain. In both seasons, His grace is more than enough. He is always near, ready to renew your strength, refresh your spirit, and remind you that you were chosen for this beautiful calling.

As you pour your heart into your children and your home, remember to care for your own soul. Take moments to pause, breathe, and rest in His presence. Whether in the chaos, the stillness, or everything in between, His grace will meet you right where you are.

May you walk forward with hope, courage, and joy, confident that the same God who entrusted you with your family, will equip and sustain you every step of the way.

You've got this, Mama, and even more importantly, God's got you.

With love and prayers,

Naphtalie Variste